I0469872

# The Land Conservancy of McHenry County

# 2015 Photo Contest

Art of the Land Amateur Photography Contest Catalog

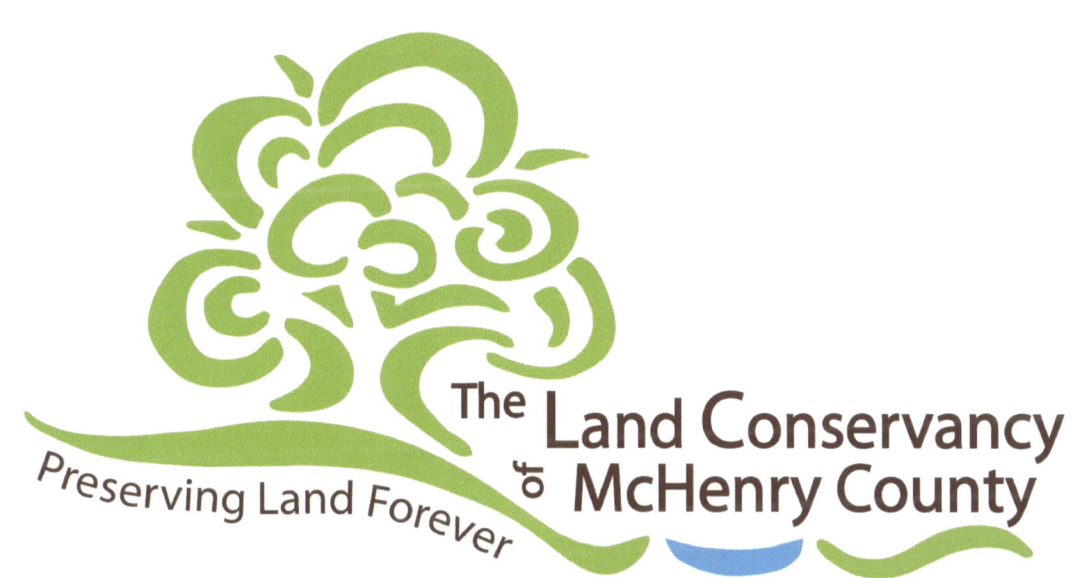

## The Mission:

To preserve natural, agricultural, and scenic land forever in and around McHenry County by working with landowners, communities and other like-minded parties.

# About The Land Conservancy of McHenry County

The Land Conservancy of McHenry County (TLC) has worked with over 100 landowners to preserve over 2,100 acres of land across McHenry County. Protected properties range from less than 1 acre to 250 acres in size. Preserved lands include high quality wetland and woodland habitat, farmland, scenic vistas, historic farmsteads, and similar valuable land resources.

The organization accomplishes most of its land preservation work by working with individuals who donate permanent conservation restrictions (also called conservation easements) on their land. Occasionally, individuals donate land to TLC and, on rare occasions, TLC purchases land.

TLC is a local 501(c)(3) nonprofit organization recognized by the IRS and the State of Illinois since 1991. The organization is funded by members, grants, and fundraising events like Art of the Land.

## The Vision

The Land Conservancy of McHenry County's vision for the future of McHenry County is that this will be a community whose people take care of their home - McHenry County - by conserving land and water resources for all generations to come.

## Share the Vision!

TLC is a nonprofit, member-supported organization. Joining is easy. Just visit the website **www.ConserveMC.org** and click on "Ways to Help," or come by the office to make a membership donation. The office is located at Hennen Conservation Area, 4622 Dean Street, Woodstock. Feel free to stop in and say hello!

# Acorn Lane Conservation Area, Lake in the Hills
## *Third Place Winner*

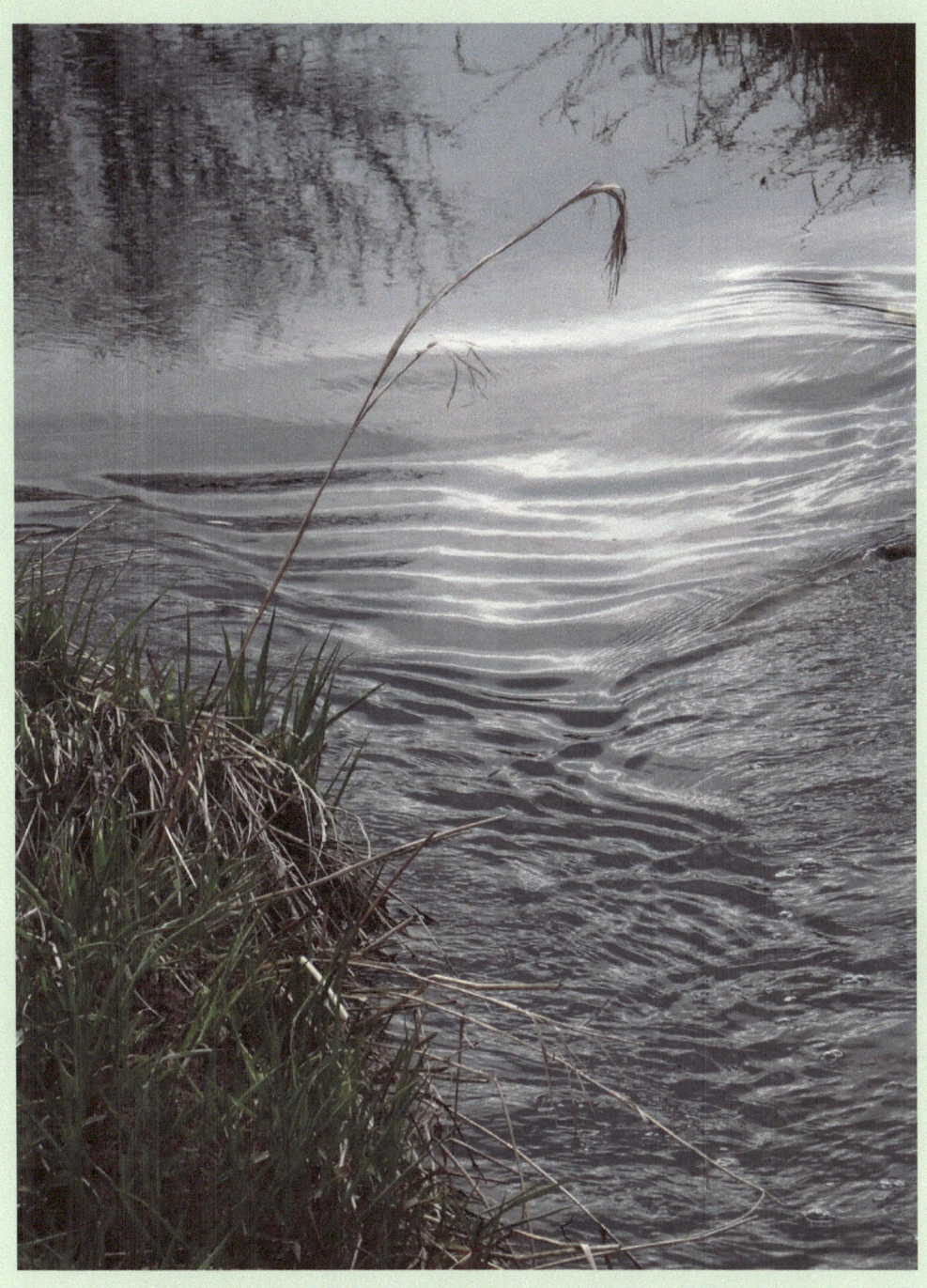

Photographer: Paul McFadden
13 acres donated to TLC in 2006

When you drive down Randall Road, you will see TLC's sign declaring "This Land is Preserved Forever!" This complex of wetlands, prairies, and recent oak plantings will always be here providing habitat and beauty.

# Acorn Lane Conservation Area, Lake in the Hills

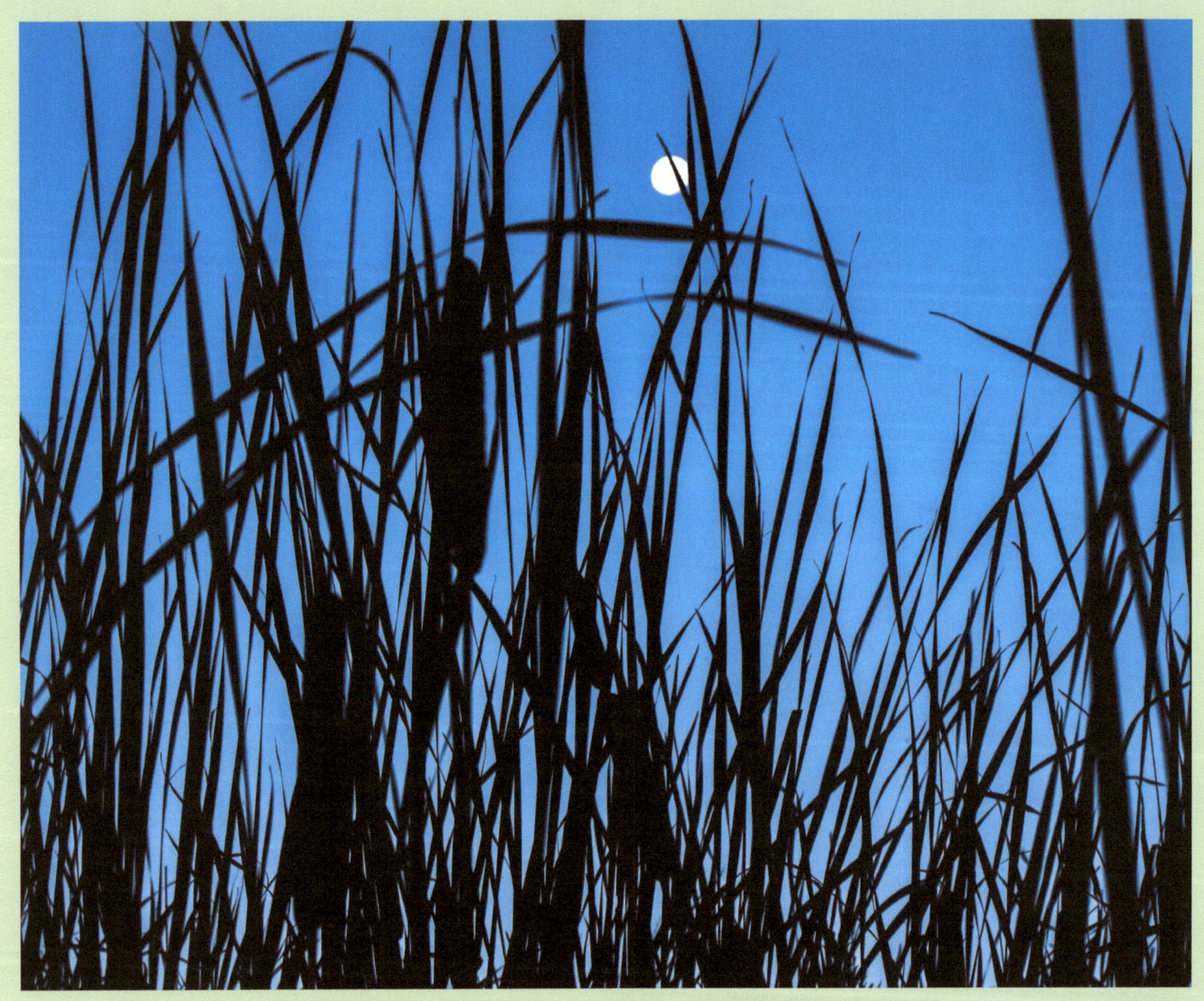

Photographer: Tom Van Der Bosch

13 acres donated to TLC in 2006

This preserve protects a section of Woods Creek and the surrounding wetland, allowing it to stay natural in a heavily developed area.

# Acorn Lane Conservation Area, Lake in the Hills
## *Honorable Mention, People's Choice*

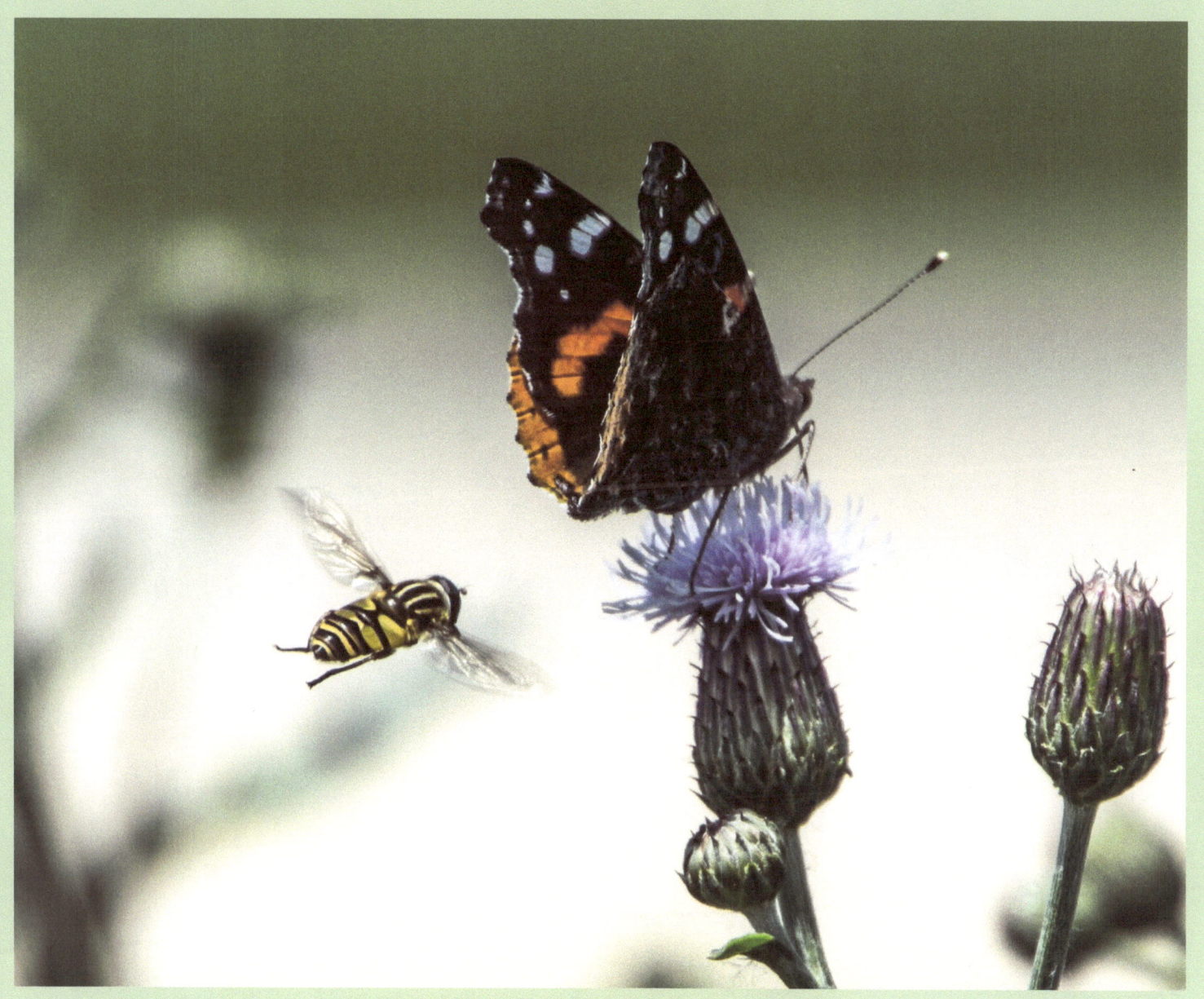

Photographer: Bob Williams
13 acres donated to TLC in 2006

At Acorn Lane, pollinators have a place to live, even along Randall Road—one of the most densely developed parts of McHenry County! That's a fly sneaking up on a red admiral butterfly—the fly only looks like a bee!

# Anderson Conservation Easement, Nunda Township

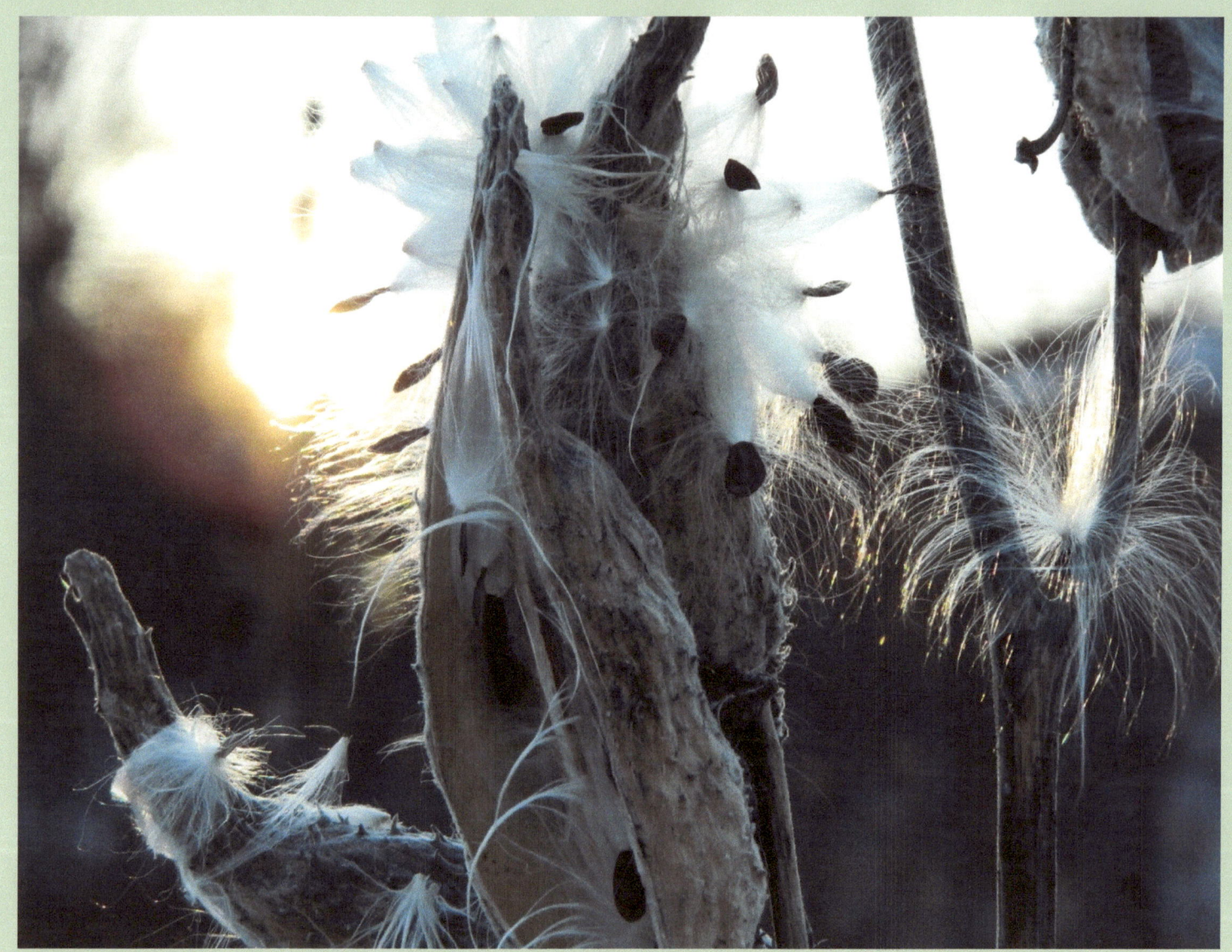

Photographer: Diana Floress

2 acres dedicated in 1994

Ders Anderson and his wife Kathe Lacey-Anderson were some of the first people in McHenry County to place a voluntary conservation easement on their property in Nunda Township, recognizing that it could be a catalyst for future preservation in the Powers Creek watershed – the largest tributary of Boone Creek, one of the highest quality streams in the state.

# Anderson Conservation Easement, Nunda Township
*Judges' Choice*

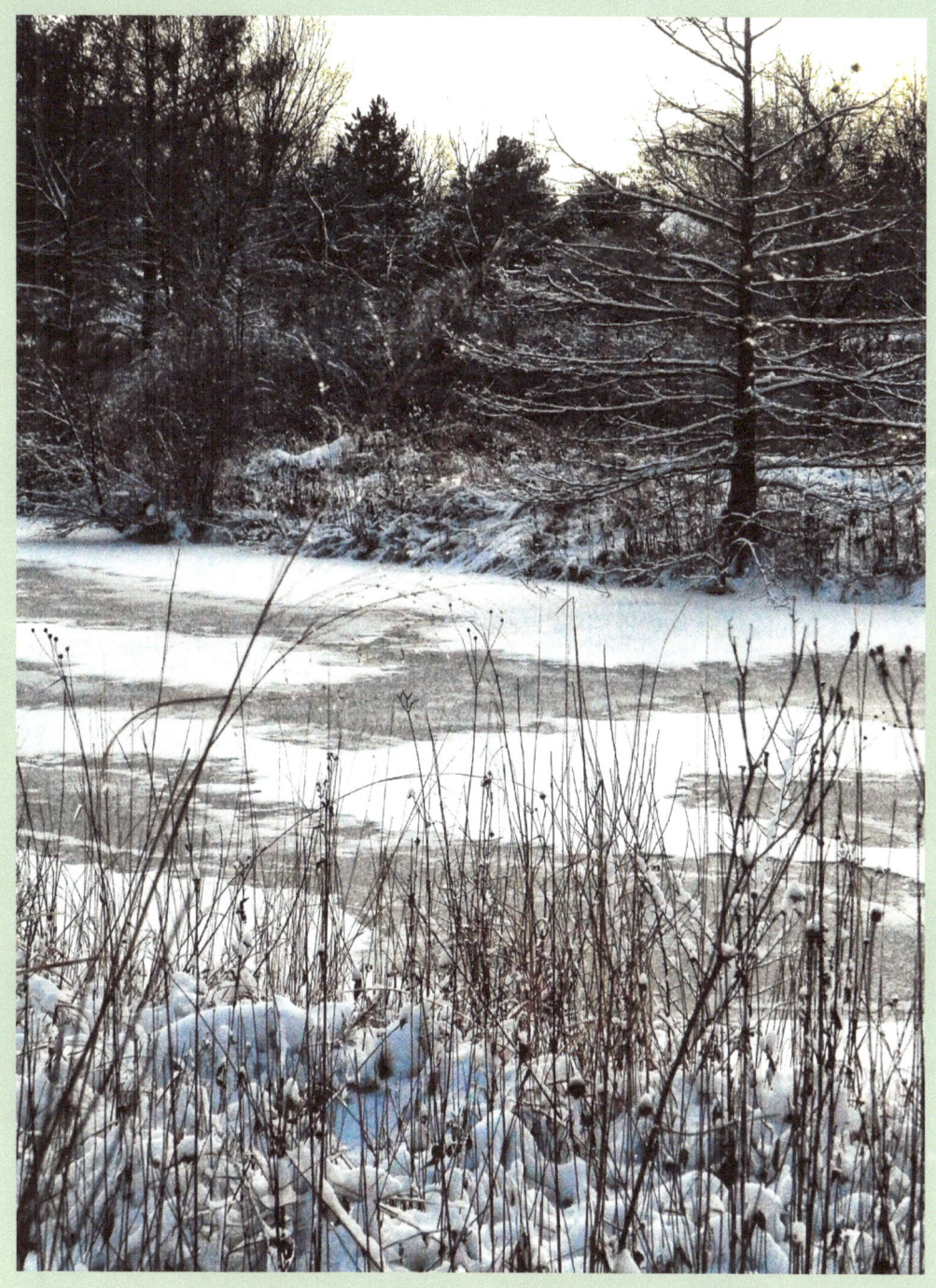

Photographer: Diana Floress

2 acres dedicated in 1994

Since the Anderson's easement was donated, an additional 300 acres of preserved land have been added to the Powers Creek corridor by TLC through conservation easements and land donations. Some catalyst!

# Apple Creek Conservation Easement, Woodstock

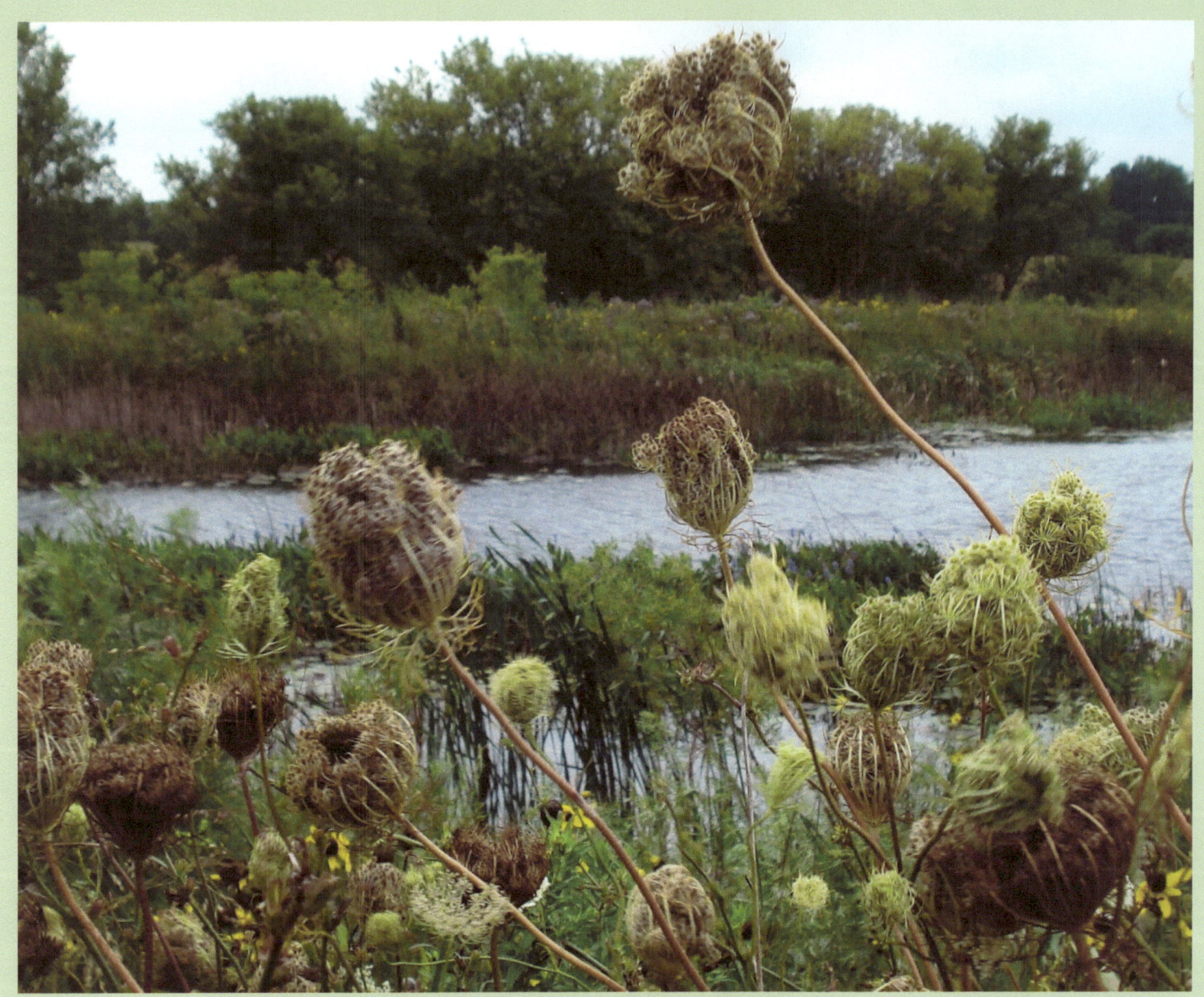

**Photographer: Pam Johnson**
**36 acres dedicated in 2007**

Apple Creek is a headwaters stream in the Kishwaukee River system, and its preservation and restoration will help maintain the high water quality in that important regional resource. As the land is restored, the Conservation Easement at Apple Creek Estates will help ensure the stream will provide high quality habitat for a diversity of wetland and upland species.

# Apple Creek Conservation Easement, Woodstock
## *Judges' Choice*

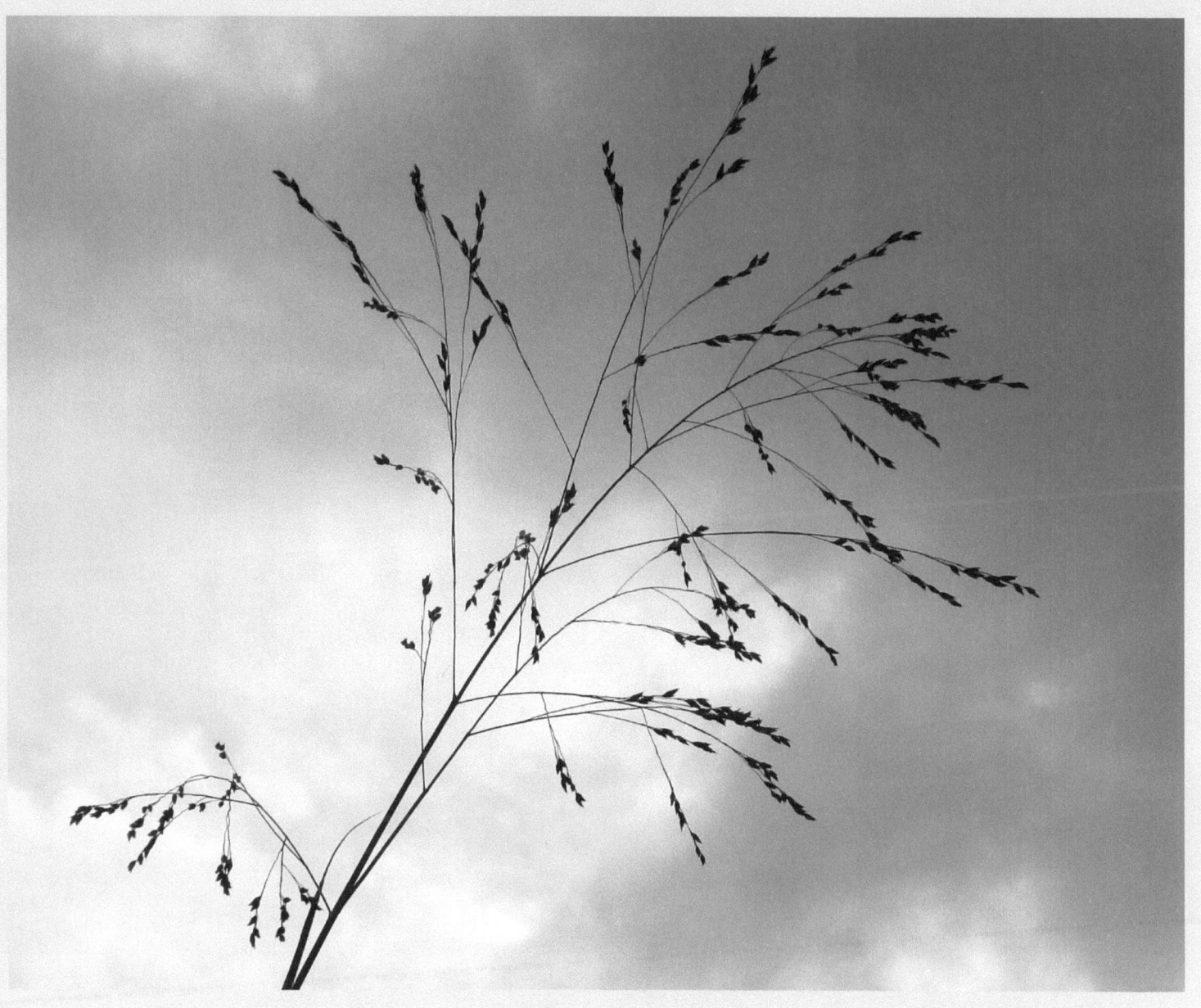

**Photographer: Pam Johnson**
**36 acres dedicated in 2007**

The conservation easement at Apple Creek Estates is one way that TLC's Vision for McHenry County will be accomplished. With two schools in the midst of the development, the conservation areas will provide ready access to nature for generations of Woodstock youth!

# Bangert Conservation Easement, Alden Township

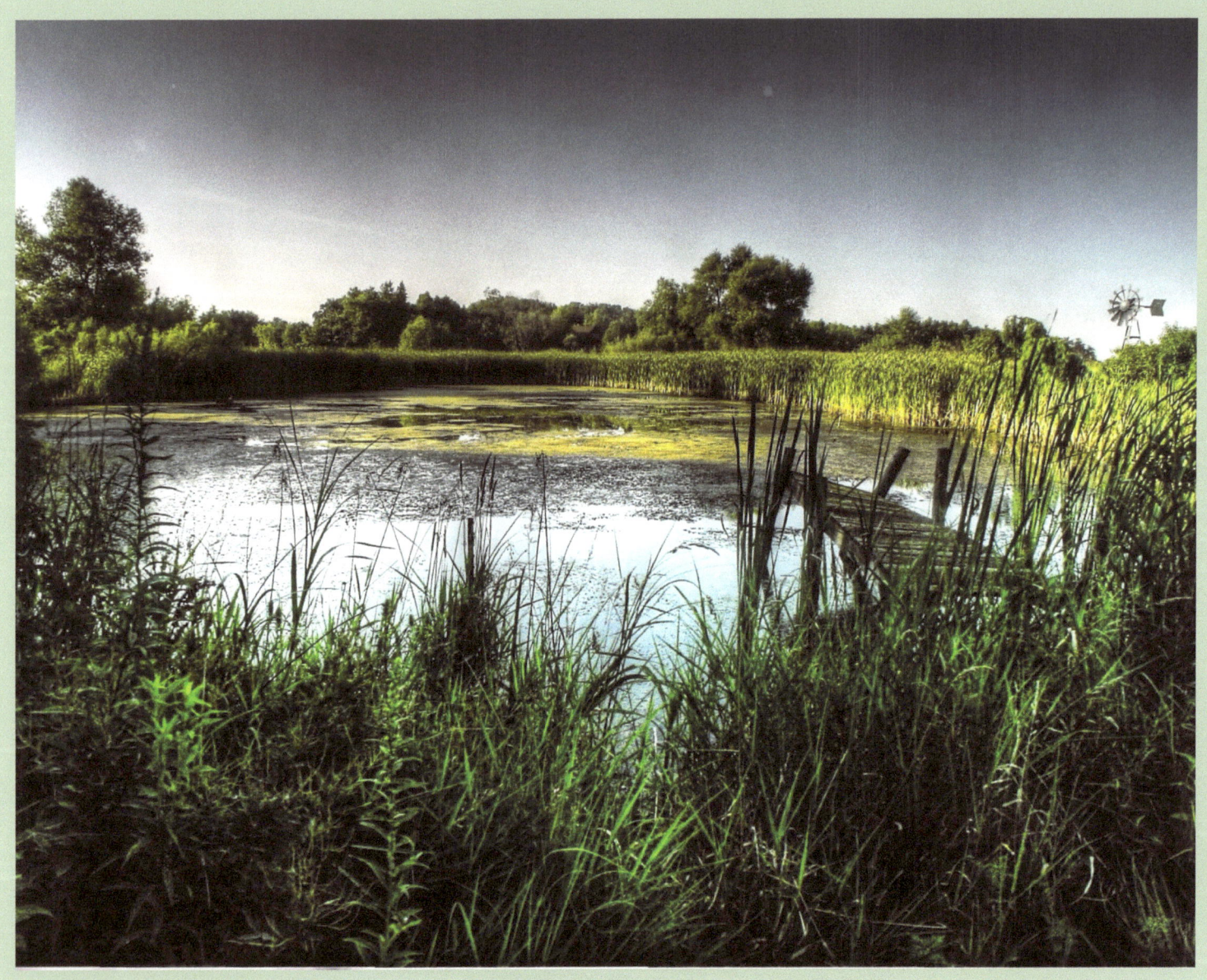

Photographer: Rob Peterson

17 acres dedicated in 2007

Orrin and Patricia Bangert have worked hard over the years, not only to restore their land in Alden Township, but also to help many of their neighbors restore habitat on their properties in the area known today as "High Point" for the presence of the highest glaciated point in Illinois (1189 feet above sea level). The commitment of the Bangerts and their neighbors to restoration resulted in MCCD's purchase of 250 acres of land that is called "High Point Conservation Area."

# Barefoot Savanna Conservation Area, Seneca Township

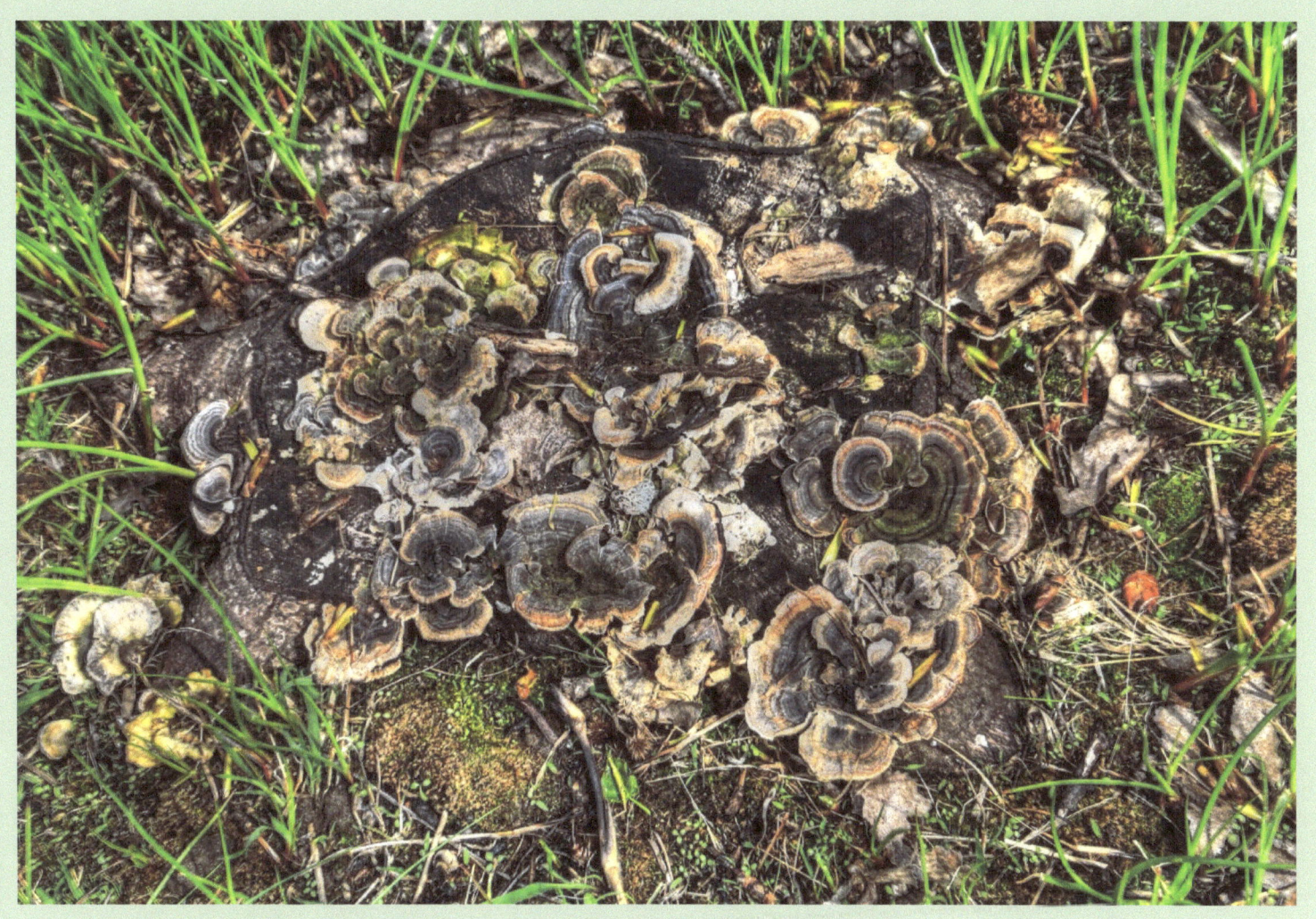

Photographer: Mike McGuigan

30 acres donated in 2013

This property was donated by Eric Tauck in 2013. Lots of work has been put into the land to transition it from farmland to a beautiful prairie and savanna where color abounds at all times of the year!

# Crowley Sedge Meadow, Alden

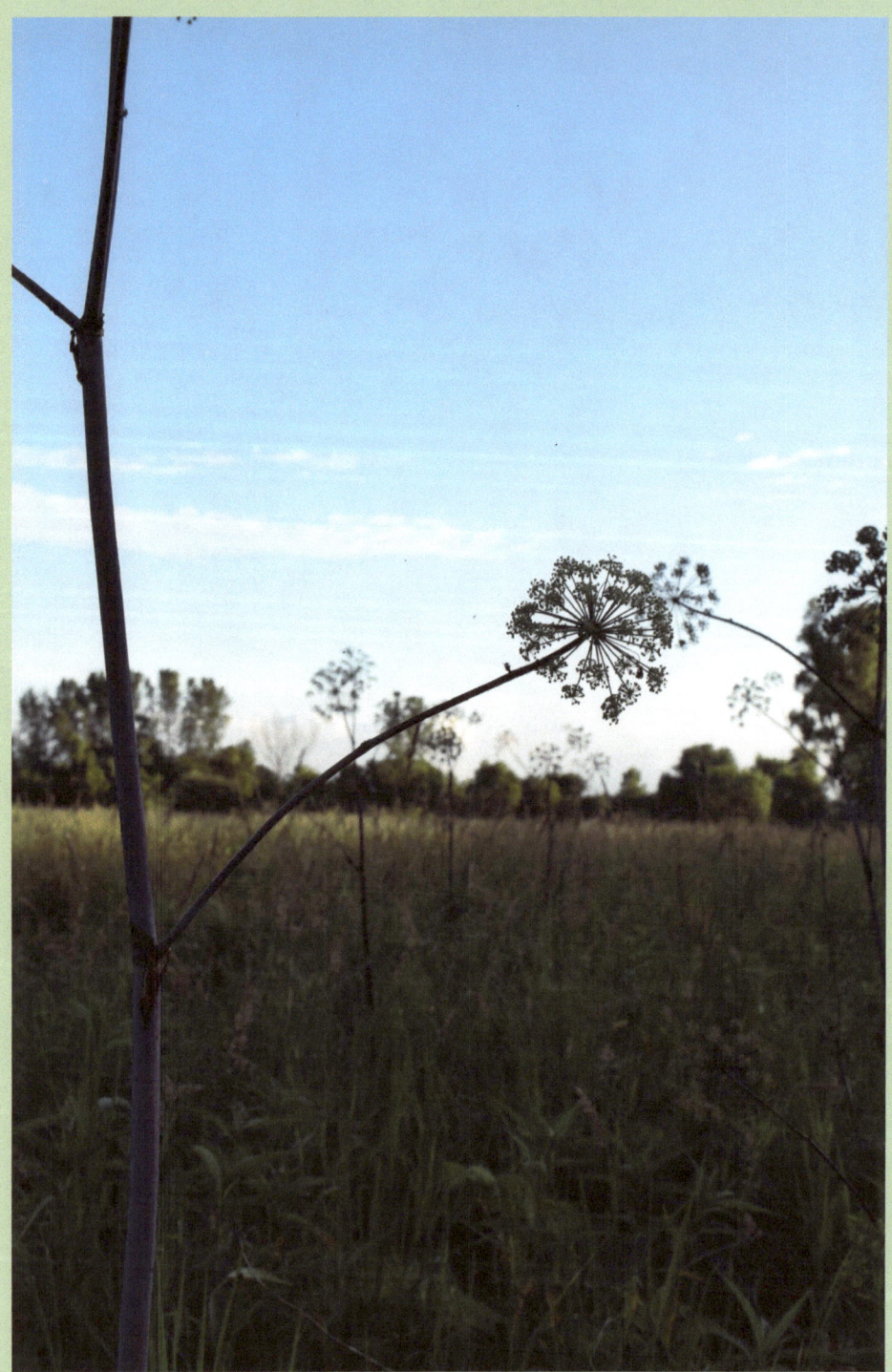

Photographer: Shawn Kingzette

6.7 acres purchased by TLC in 2004

Crowley Sedge Meadow is the first land that TLC purchased. TLC secured a mortgage to protect this remnant that was too small and isolated for a government agency to buy. Many hours have gone towards brush clearing, weed pulling, prescribed fires, and oak plantings. This little sedge meadow really shines now!

# Dutch Creek Conservation Easement, Johnsburg
## *Honorable Mention*

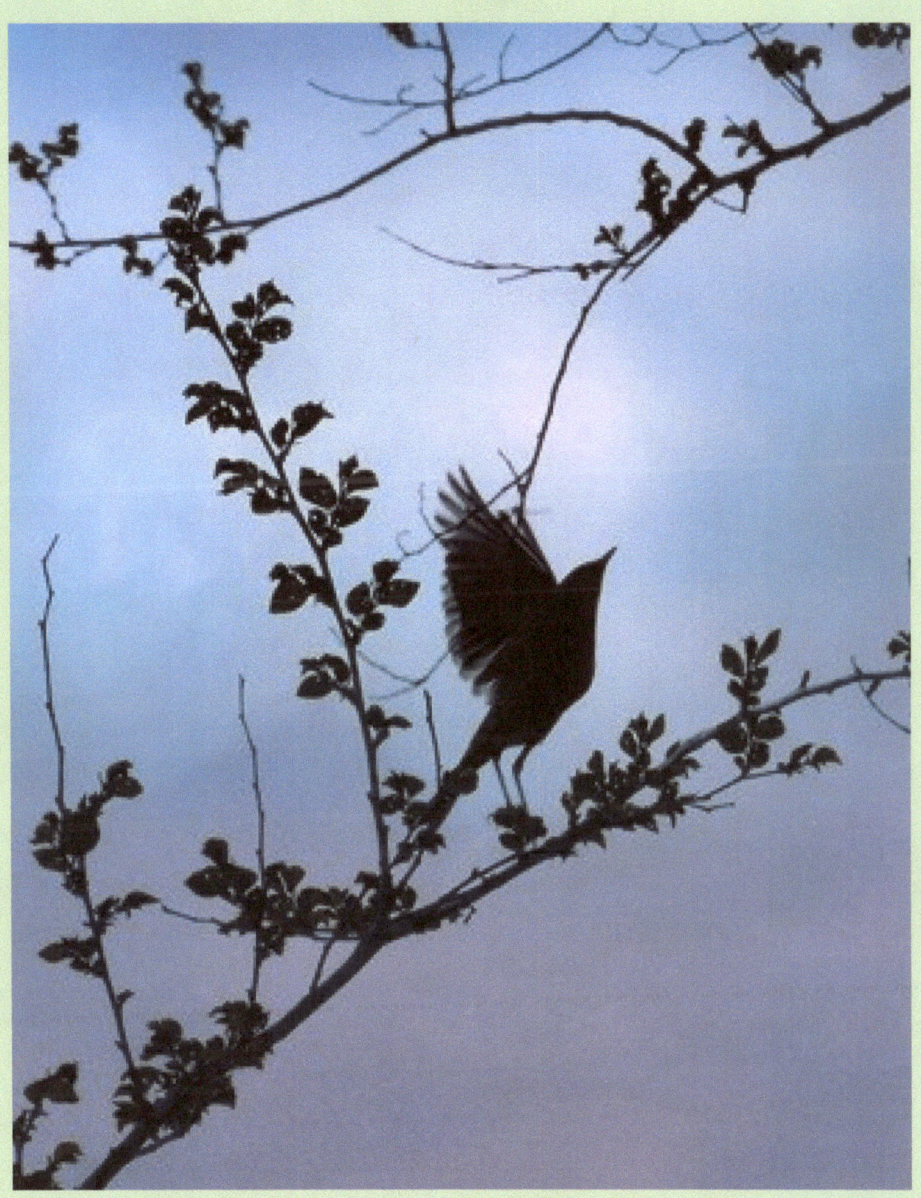

Photographer: Caroline Flaherty
60 acres dedicated in 2007

This easement, located within the Dutch Creek Estates subdivision. It protects 170 native plant species that call this their home.

# Dutch Creek Conservation Easement, Johnsburg

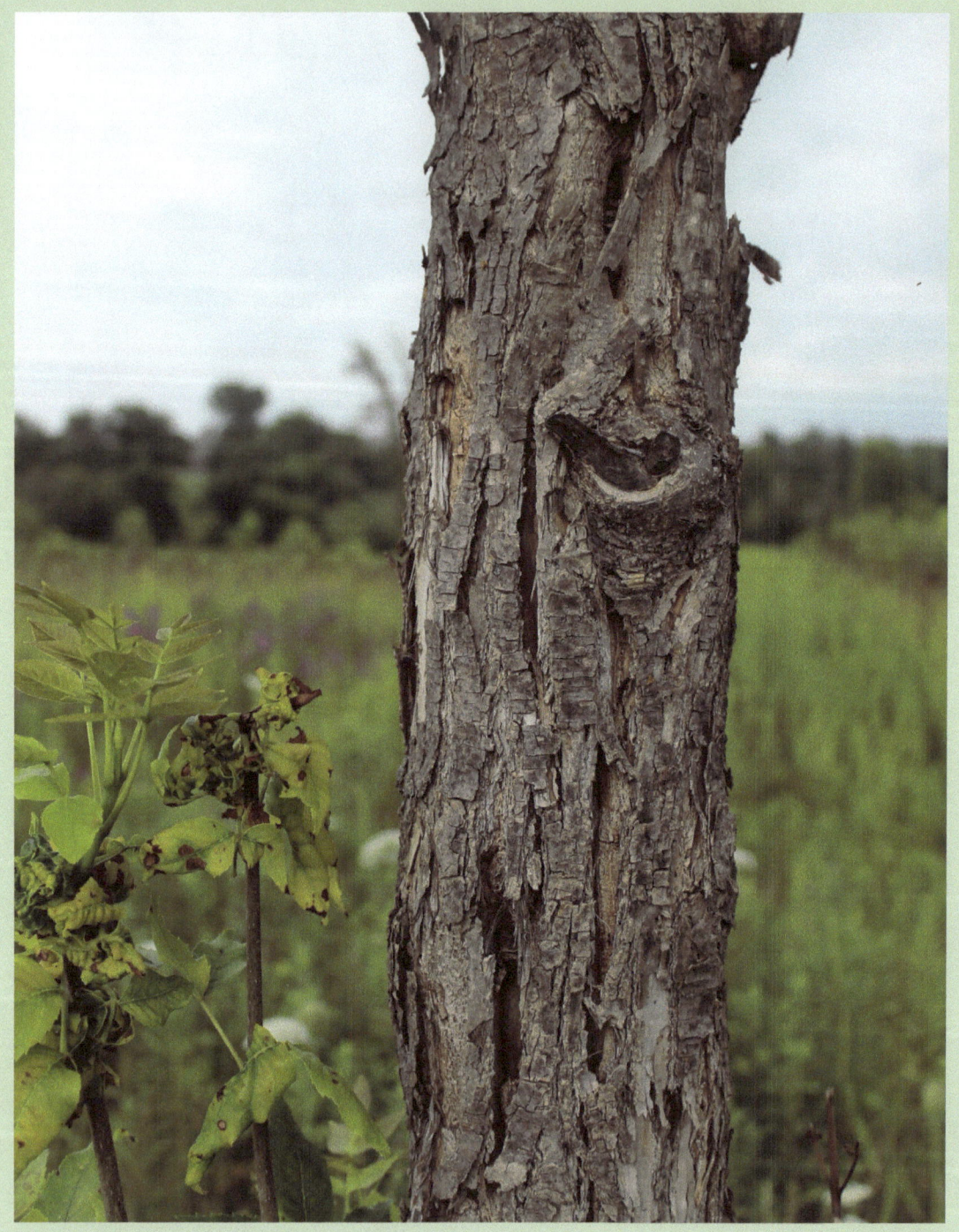

Photographer: Danica Garcia

60 acres dedicated in 2007

Dutch Creek is one of the highest quality headwater streams in the county. The stream flows through sedge meadows, fens, and oak woods. Students from the local junior high have planted oaks each Arbor Day for the past six years — over 300 oaks in 7 years!

# Harvard Gateway Nature Park

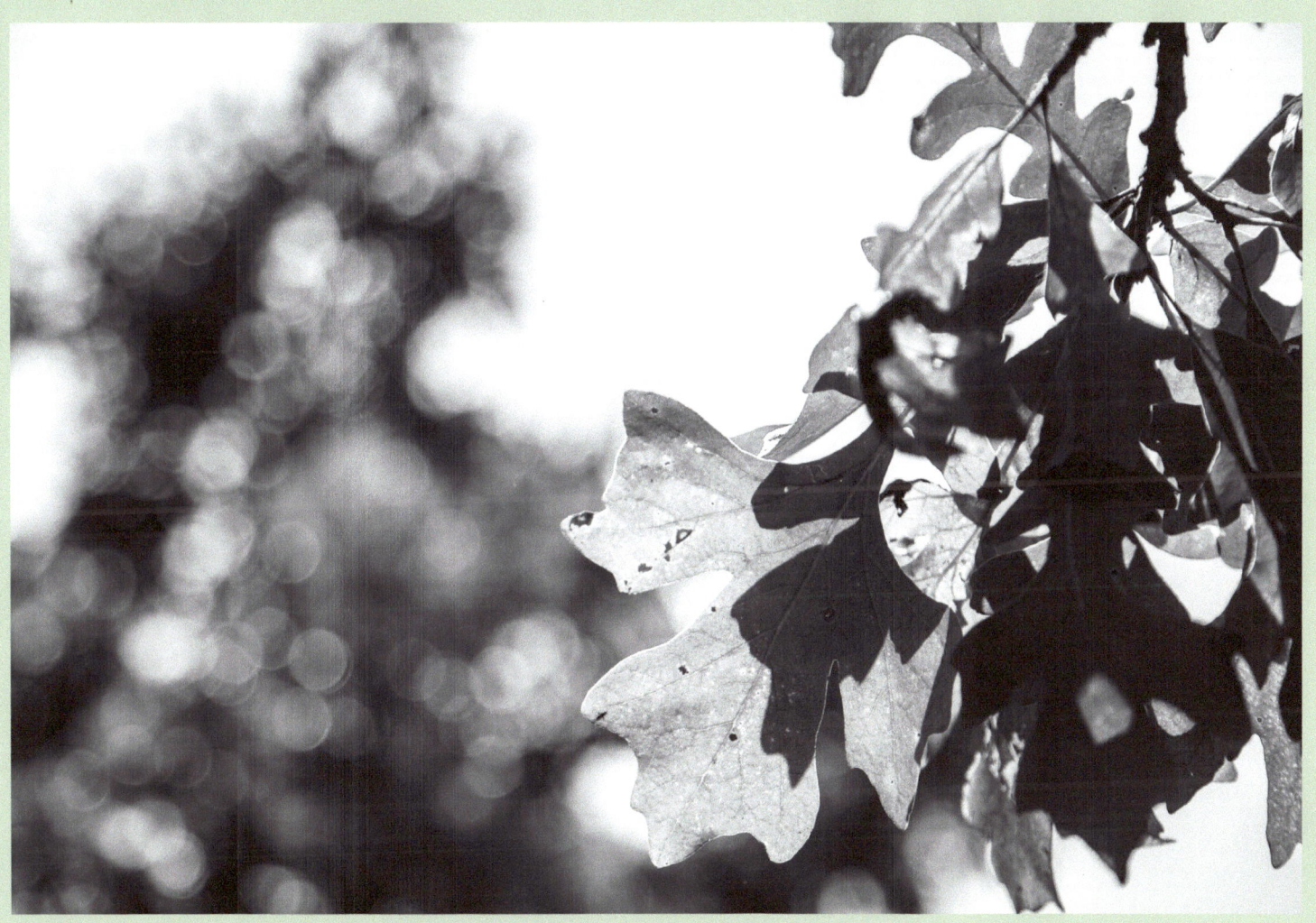

Photographer: Jackie Alvarado

17.5 acres purchased in 2012

When TLC acquired this site we discovered a true gem: the county's largest white oak, estimated to be 400 years old. Now that most of the invasive brush has been removed, the oak limbs can spread out and reach for the abundant sunlight.

# Harvard Gateway Nature Park

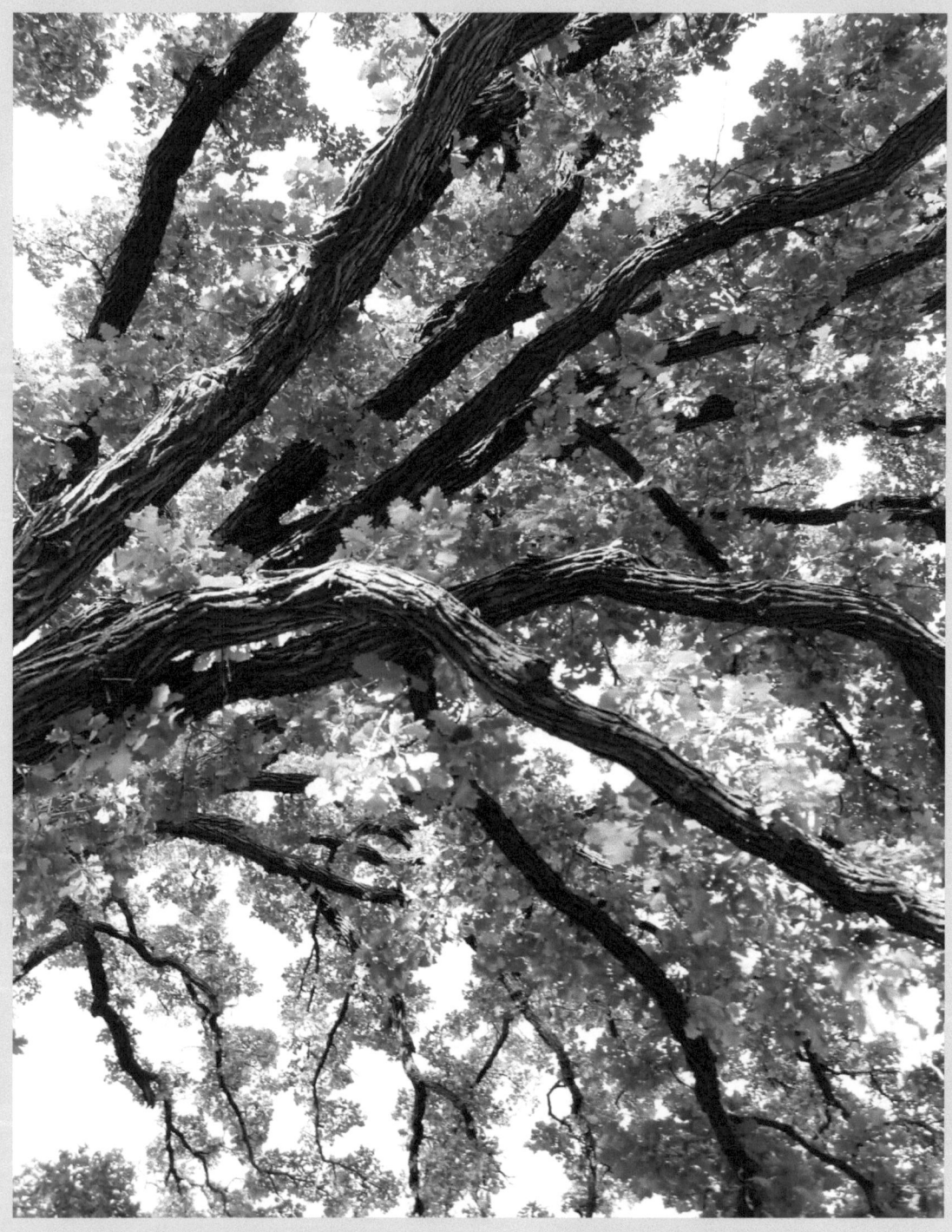

Photographer: Elinor Stark

17.5 acres purchased in 2012

Little treasures keep popping up at this site as restoration continues.
Each year the prairies, savannas, and wetlands offer new and
exciting views and a great diversity of color. The open woodland now
invites uncommon species like bluebirds!

# Pensinger Conservation Easement

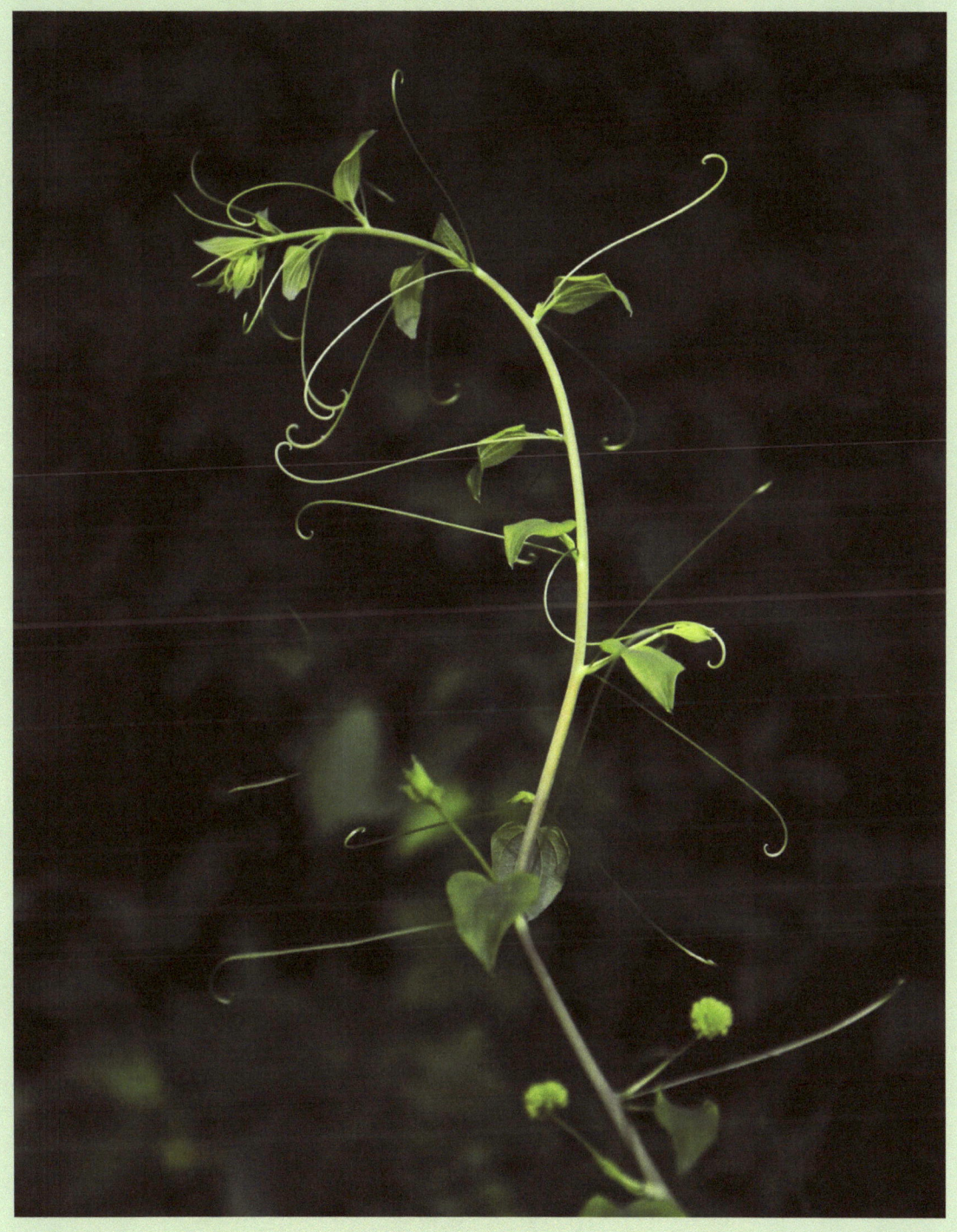

Photographer: Margie Bjorkman

3 acres dedicated in 2009

Lynn and Ray Pensinger live amidst a beautiful oak woodland on Fleming Road near Bull Valley, a property adjacent to TLC's 149 acre Finch Farm Conservation Easement. After years of hard work restoring their woods, they decided to make sure that the woods would be preserved forever The woods will be home to people, plants and wildlife forever.

# Pistakee Preserve, McHenry Township

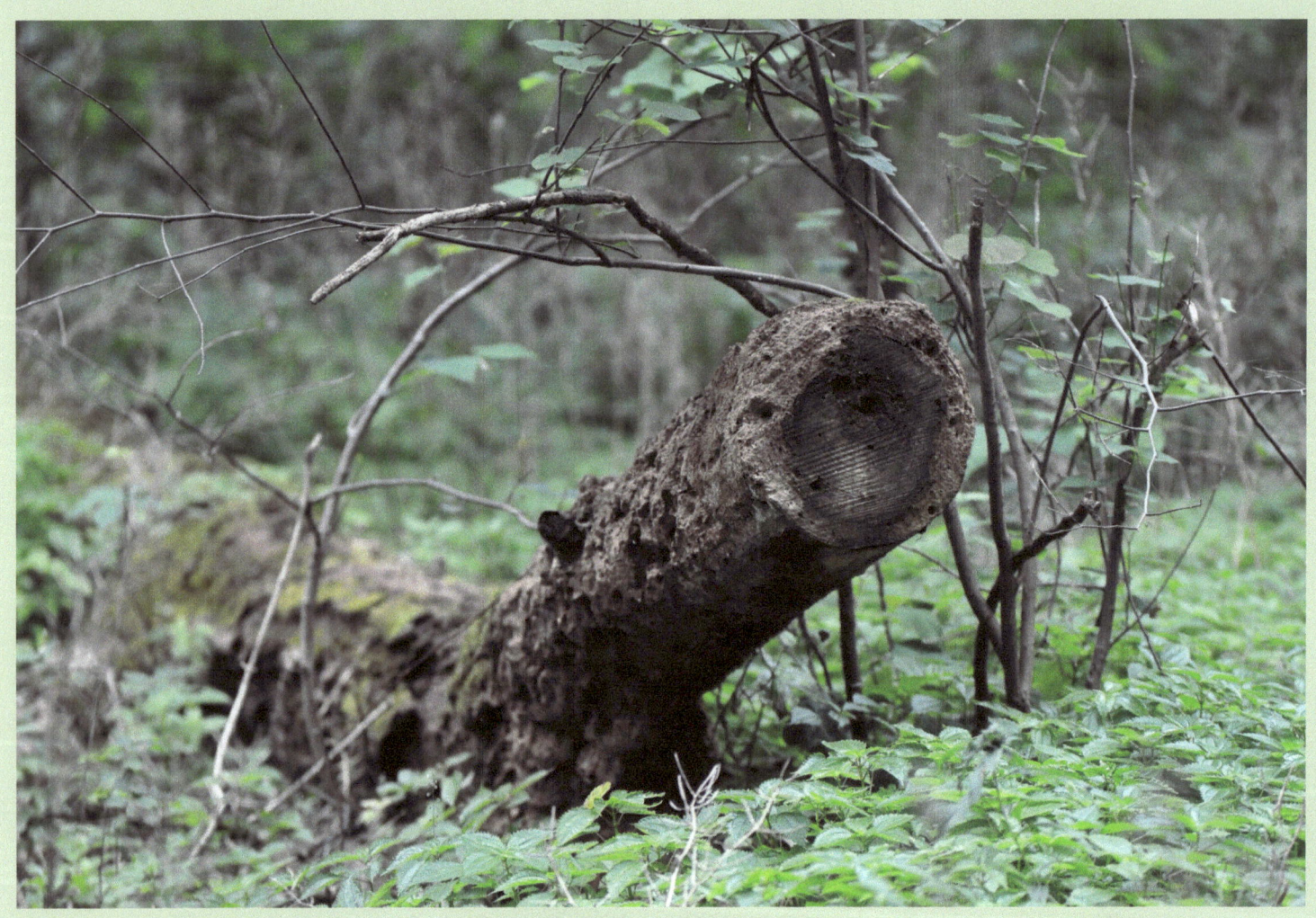

Photographer: Bud Lawrence

3 acres donated in 2009

This land along Pistakee Lake has been in the same family since the 1800s. The three Olson sisters agreed on a donation to TLC, protecting the natural lakeshore and a lagoon in an area where mowed lawns line most of the lake.

# Powers Creek Conservation Area, Bull Valley
*Second Place*

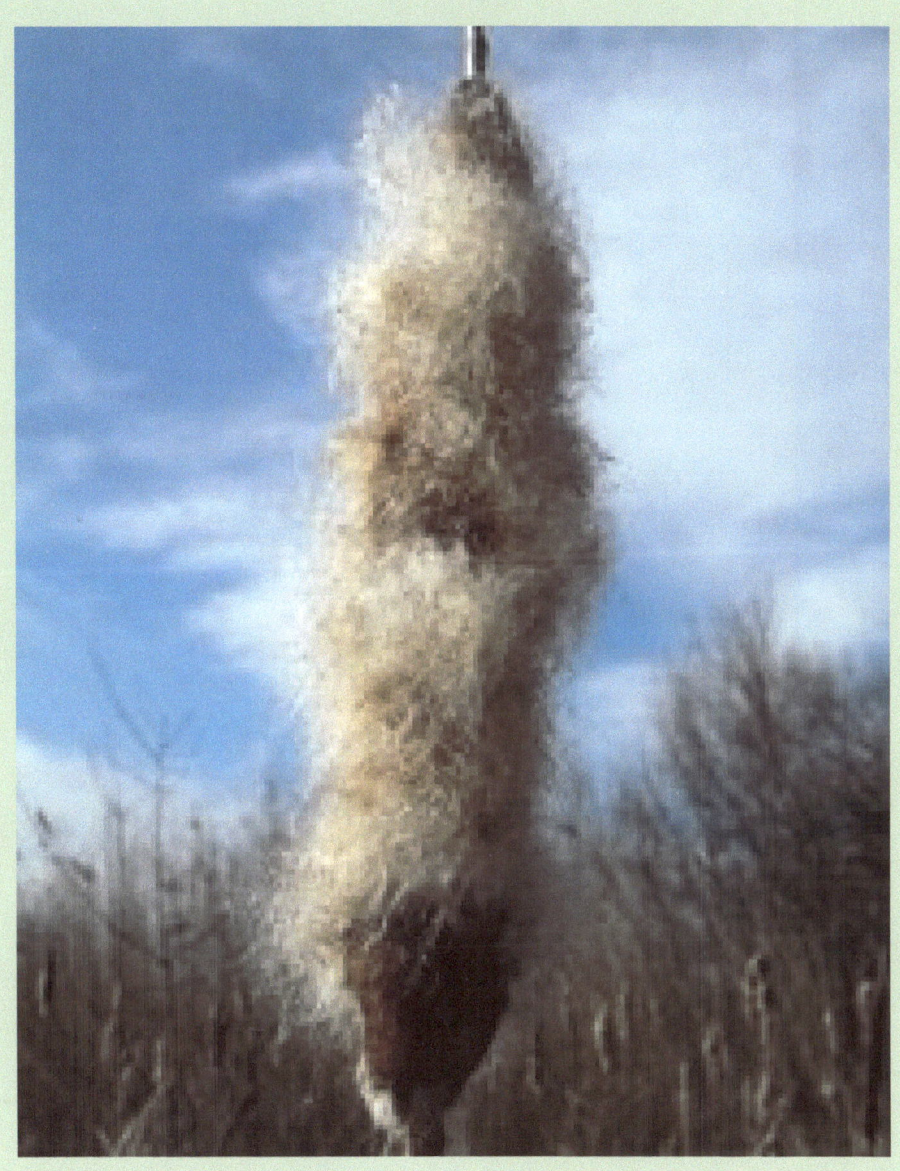

## Photographer: Kendal Stephens
### 22 acres donated in 2002

The property includes a portion of Powers Creek (a tributary to
Boone Creek), as well as two upland seeps in the Windy Knoll
Estates subdivision. With regular management that includes clearing
of invasive brush and use of ecological fire, the site provides
important habitat for a diversity of plant, animal and insect species.

# Remington Grove Conservation Easement, Johnsburg

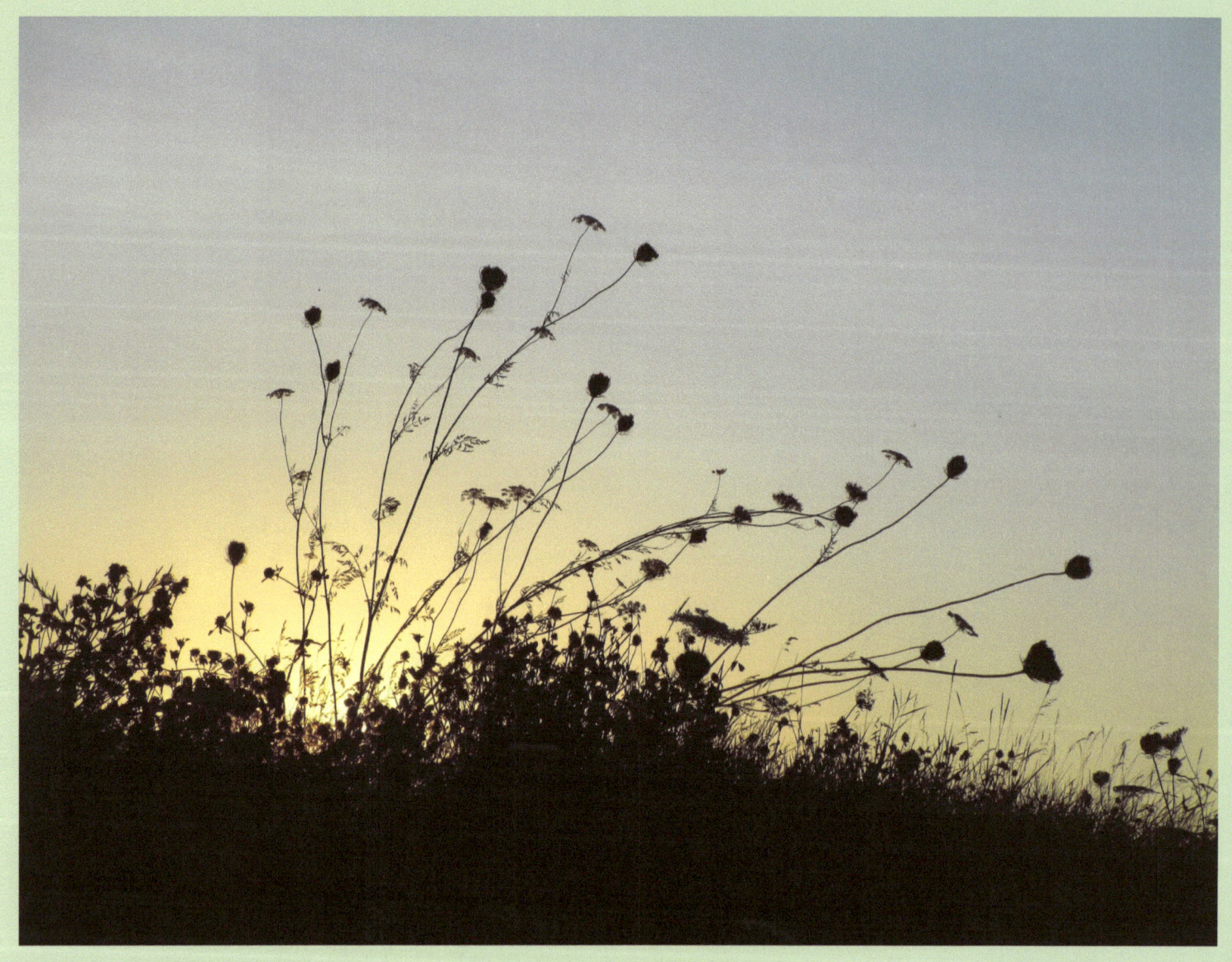

Photographer: MaryJo Stedman

23 acres dedicated in 2012

This property is located in the west branch of Dutch Creek, providing an important buffer to the creek as well as nice restored wetlands and a prairie.

# Sobczak Conservation Easement, Greenwood

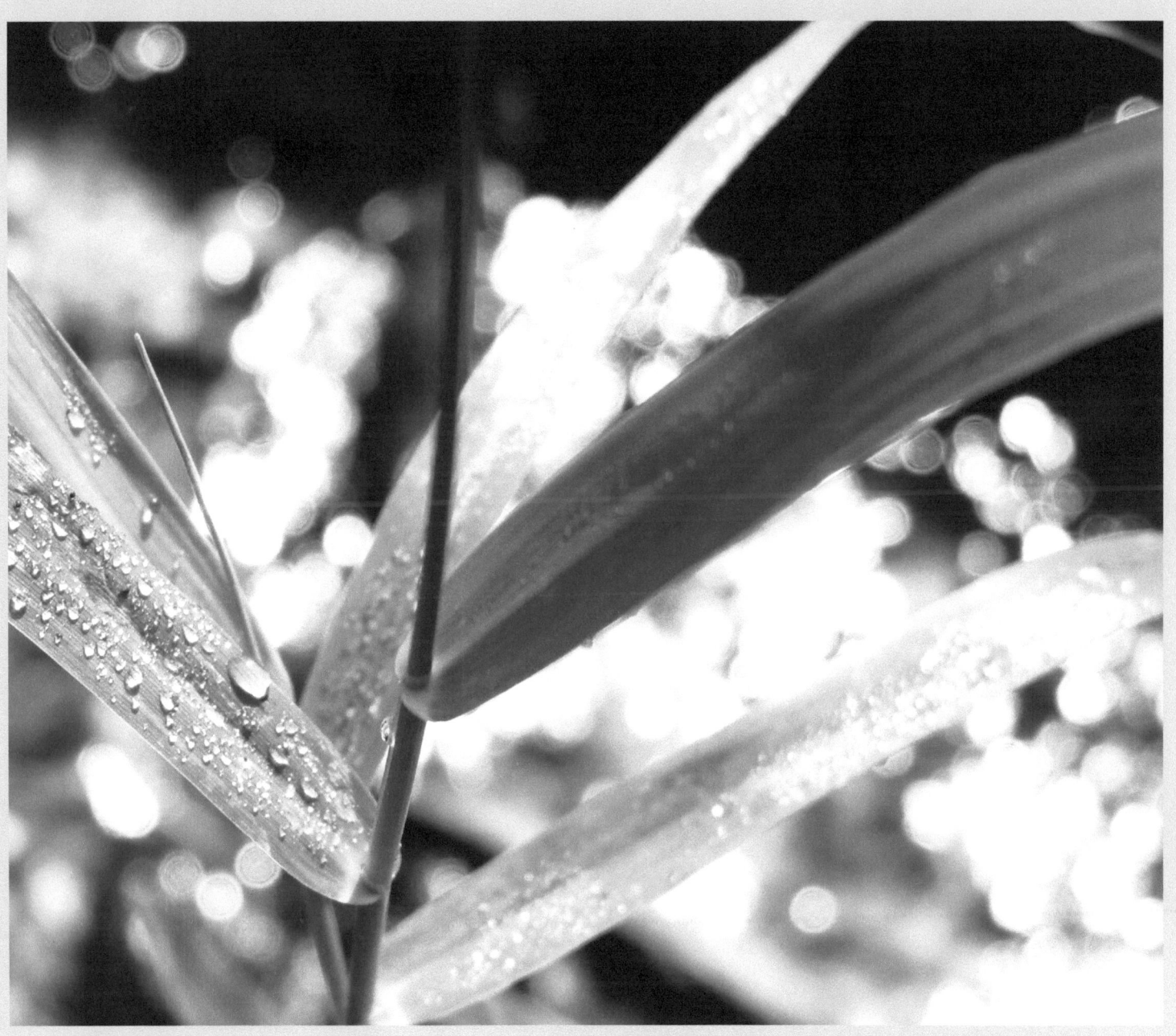

Photographer: Kathy Hammond
3.4 acres dedicated in 2008

Situated right along Nippersink Creek and adjacent to land already protected by McHenry County Conservation District, this lovely parcel extends the amount of land set aside to remain wild and beautiful and adds more protection for our important water resources.

# Simon Conservation Easement, Alden Township
## *Best Youth Photo Award*

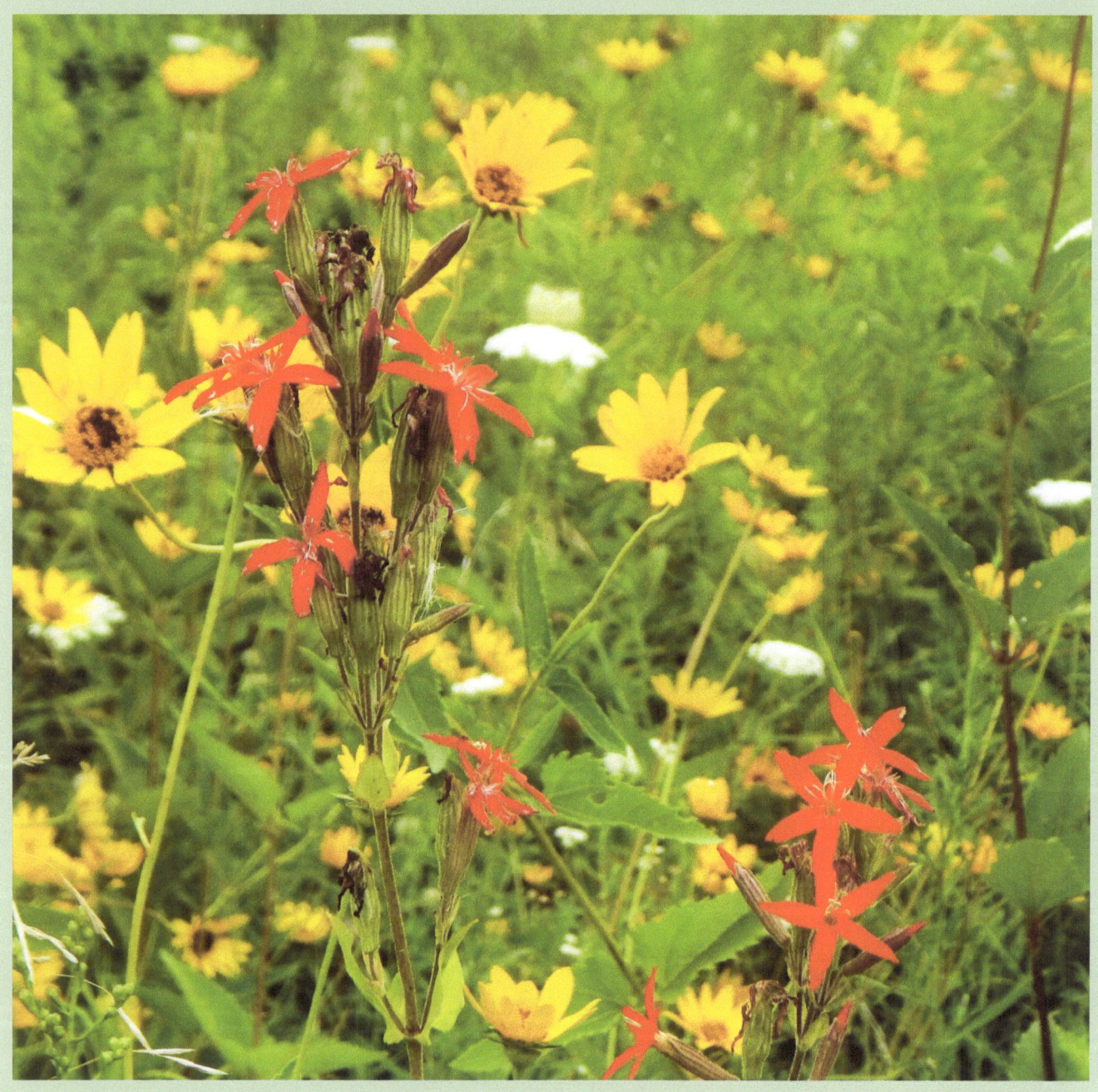

Photographer: Avril Westphal

1 acre dedicated to TLC in 2007

Stephanie and Jerry Simon acquired a beautiful piece of land with the Nippersink Creek running through it. The rolling topography offers a spectacular view of the creek and all the wildflowers blooming along it--thanks to many hours of hard work!

# Simon Conservation Easement, Alden Township
*Judges' Choice*

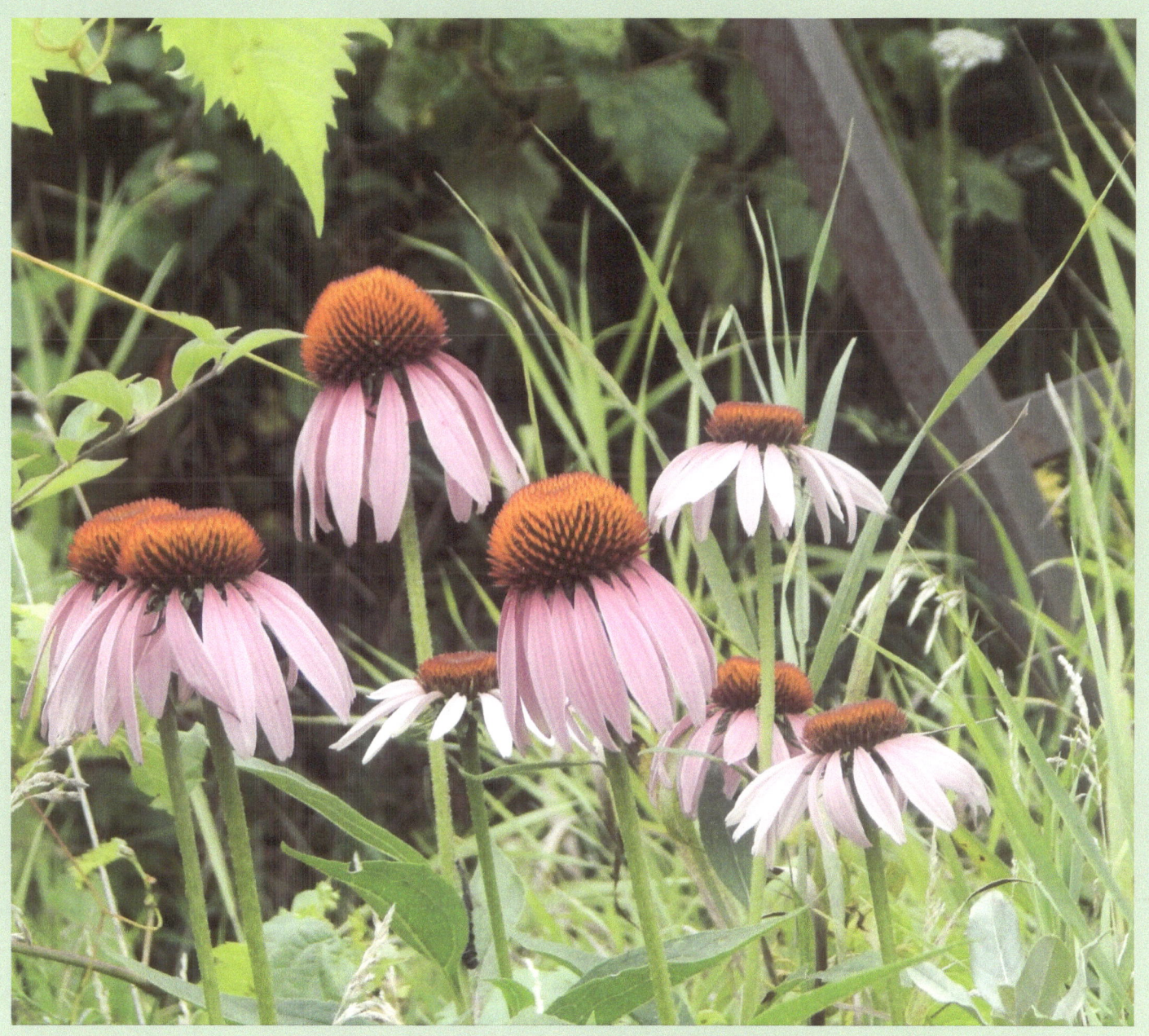

Photographer: Avril Westphal

1 acre dedicated to TLC in 2007

Jerry and Stephanie's love for the land led them to place a conservation easement with TLC on an acre that includes the creek to ensure that the work they are doing today will be preserved forever.

# Spring Hollow Conservation Easement, Bull Valley
## *Honorable Mention*

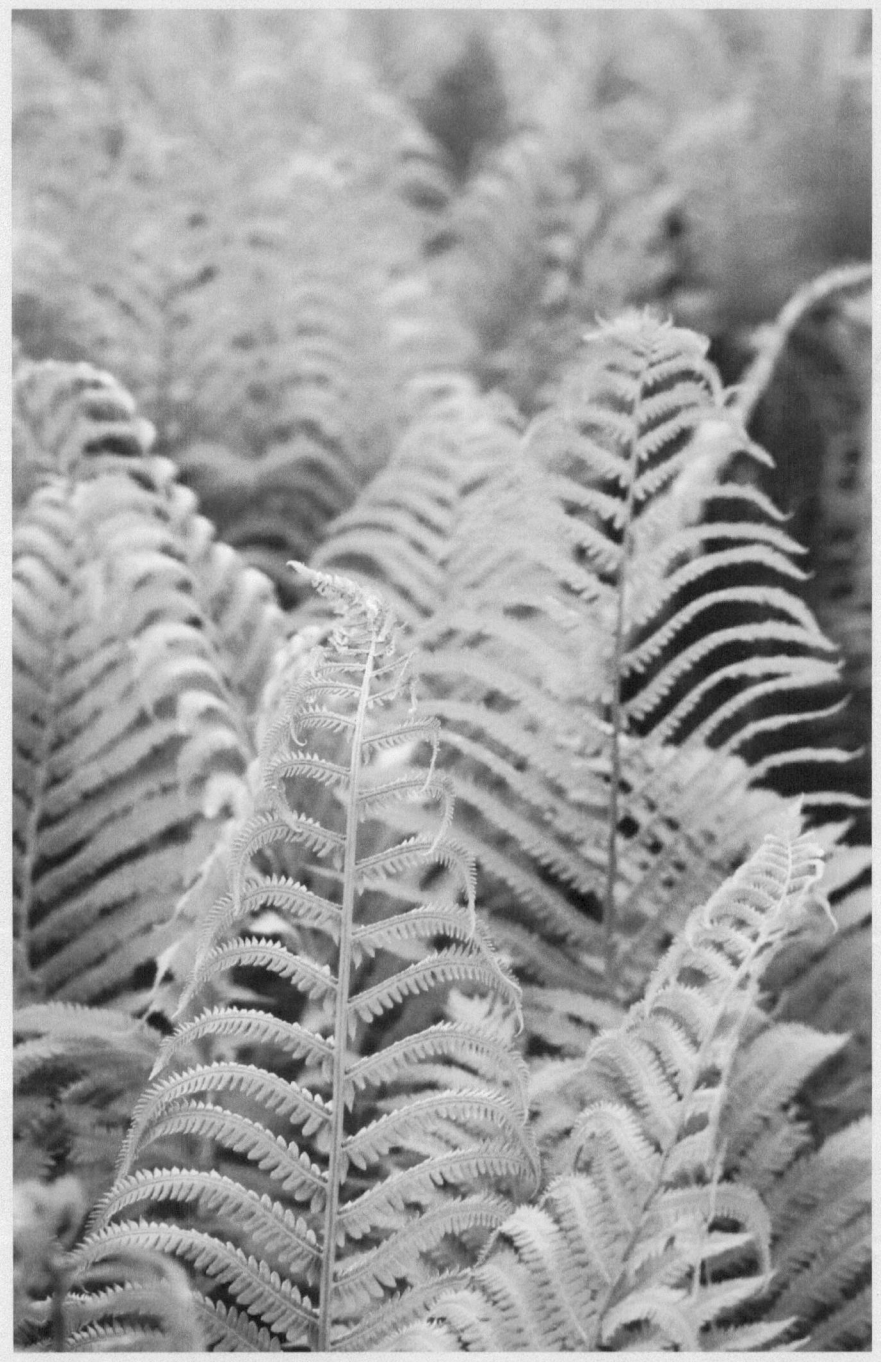

Photographer: Gail Moreland

35 acres dedicated in 1977, transferred to TLC in 2013

Dick and Betty Babcock were the first Illinois family to dedicate a permanent conservation easement on their land in December 1977, making use of the law which Dick Babcock helped create. They named this place Spring Hollow for its many natural springs and rolling topography, and it is still in the family today.

# Spring Ridge Conservation Easement, Woodstock

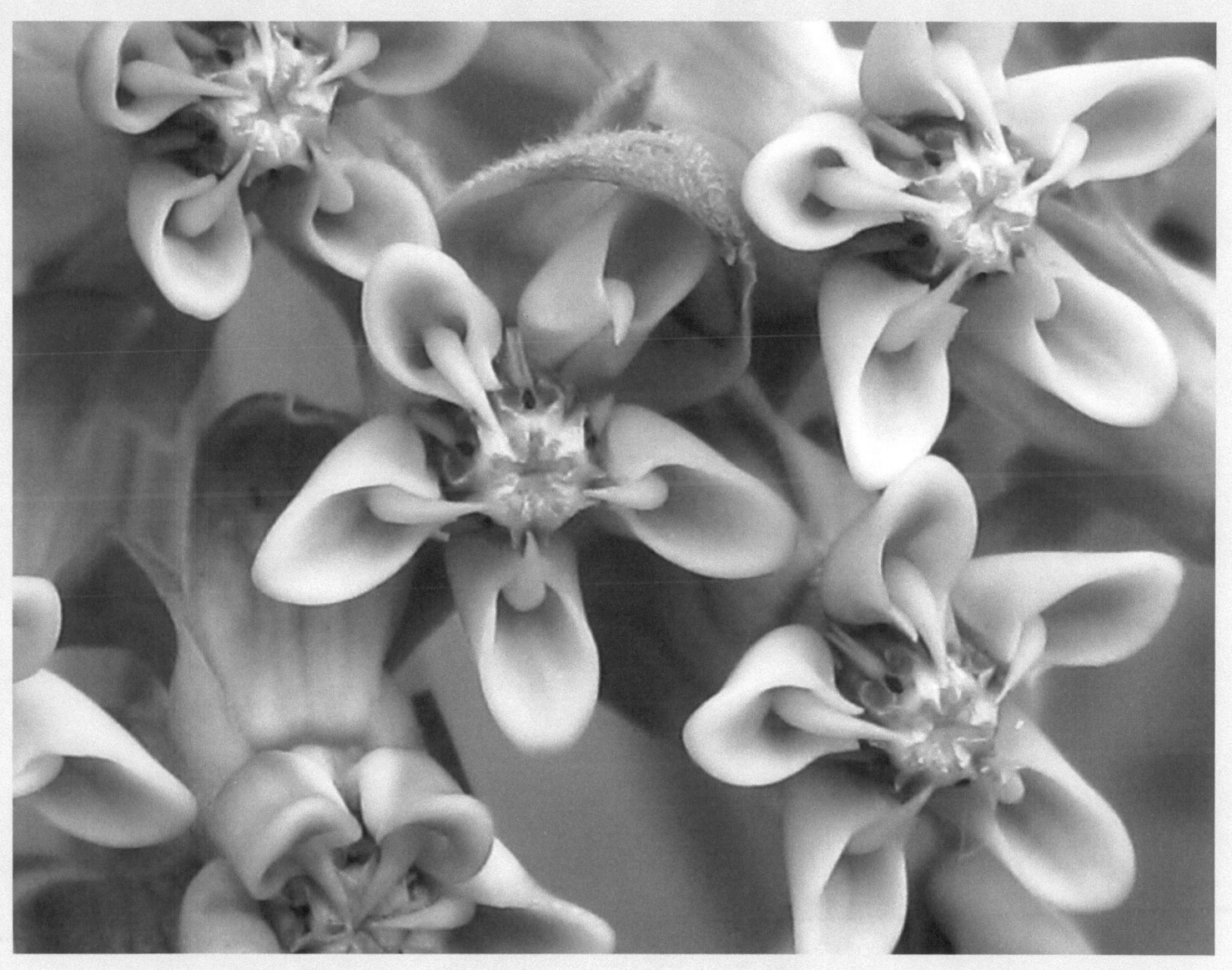

Photographer: Lauren Mirs
2 acres dedicated in 2002

The conservation easement in the Spring Ridge subdivision is part of an 11 acre greenway corridor that captures and cleans strormwater as it runs through the Country Ridge subdivision to the south and east to TLC's Concannon Conservation Area.

# Swanson Conservation Easement, Ringwood

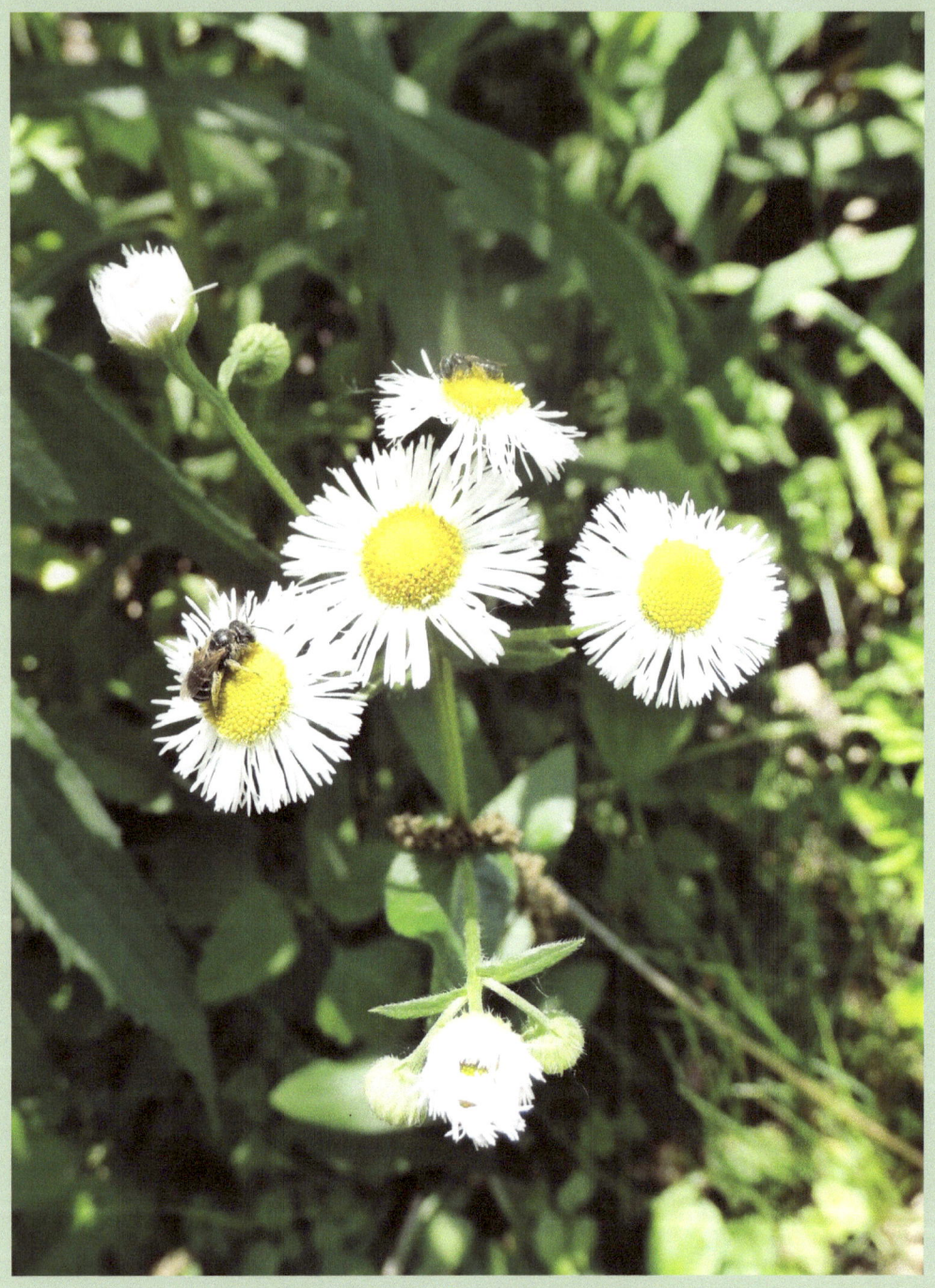

Photographer: Linda Santeler

4 acres dedicated in 2009

Paths wind through groves of oak trees and around ponds, all offering an astounding view of various spring wildflowers. Few backyards can boast the number of songbirds, frogs, and other critters that call this their home. Thanks to years of careful tending and the foresight to dedicate an easement, this yard will remain natural forever.

# Swanson Conservation Easement, Ringwood

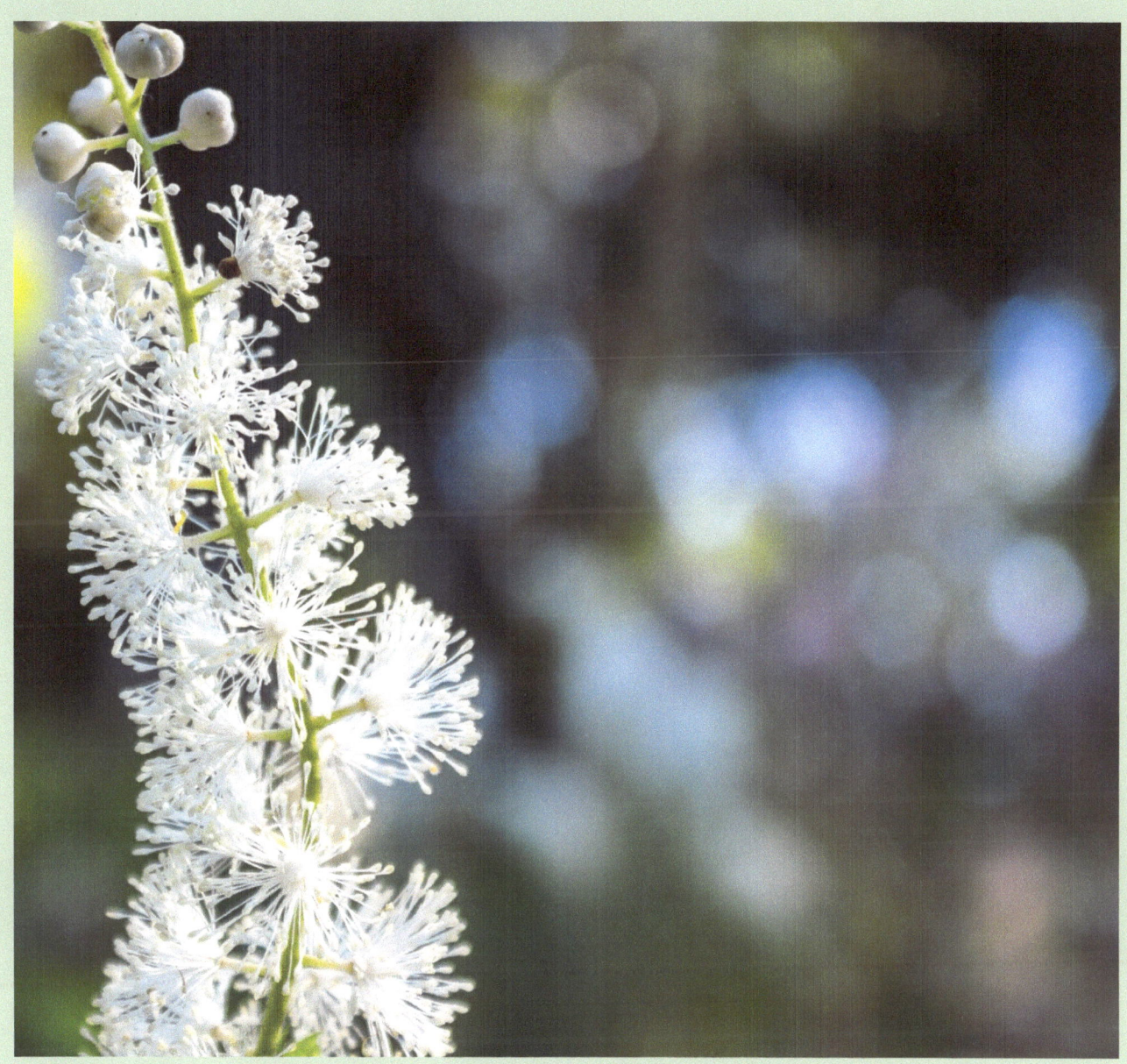

Photographer: Sheryl Smith

4 acres dedicated in 2009

The Swansons started clearing buckthorn from around their ancient oaks and shagbark hickories in 1992 when they first moved to the property in Ringwood. Today, the oak woods have a diverse understory of native flowers and shrubs, plus young oaks that will one day grow to replace the ancient ones.

# Tauck Conservation Easement, Seneca Township

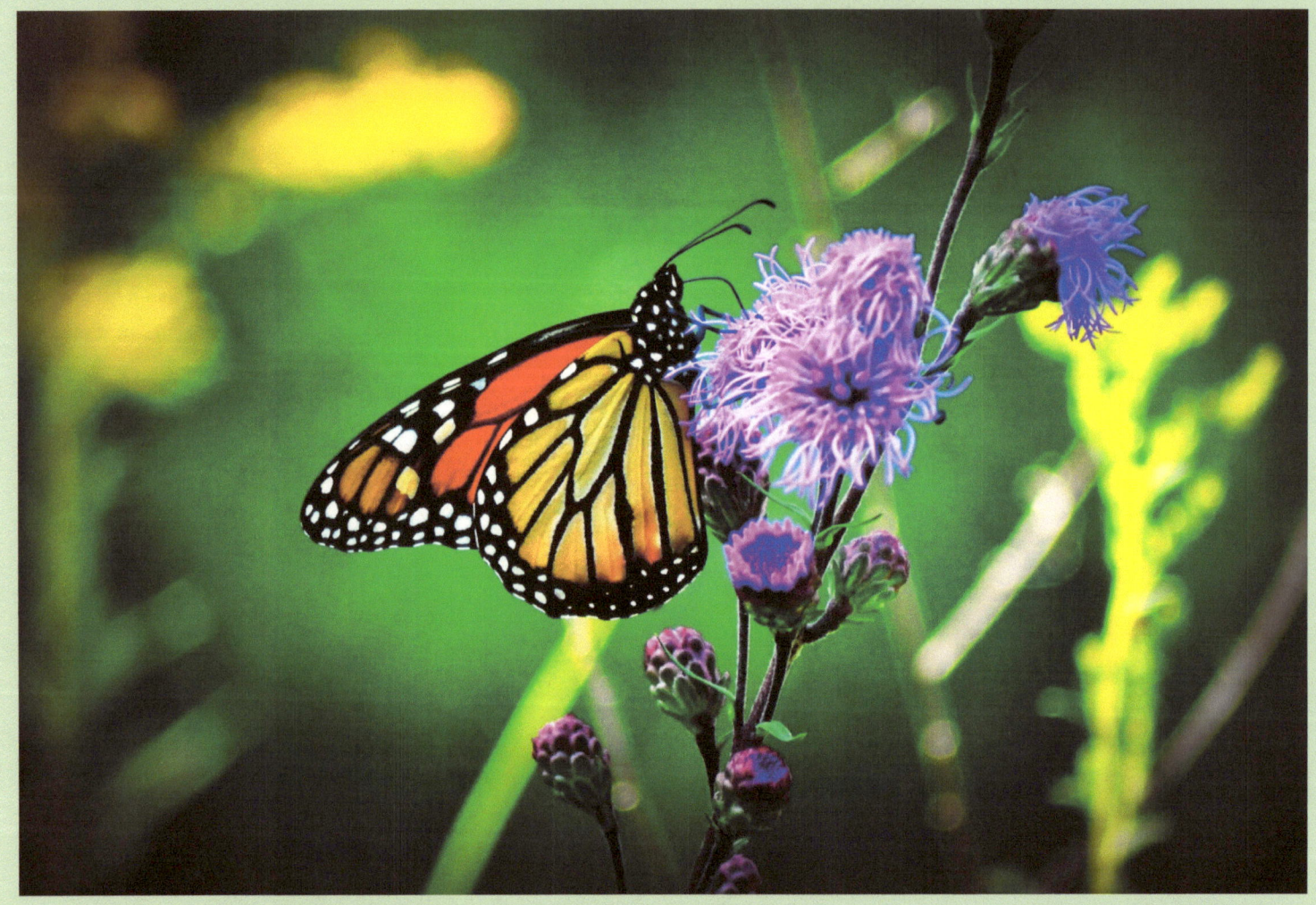

Photographer: Jennifer Luniewicz-Martins
11 acres dedicated in 1993

Thirty-three acres of prairie, oak woodland and sedge meadow will remain undeveloped forever through the two conservation easements Dorothy Weers placed on the property she owned. While Dorothy is no longer with us, her legacy lives on as the new owners continue to care for the property

# Wonder Lake Sedge Meadow, Wonder Lake

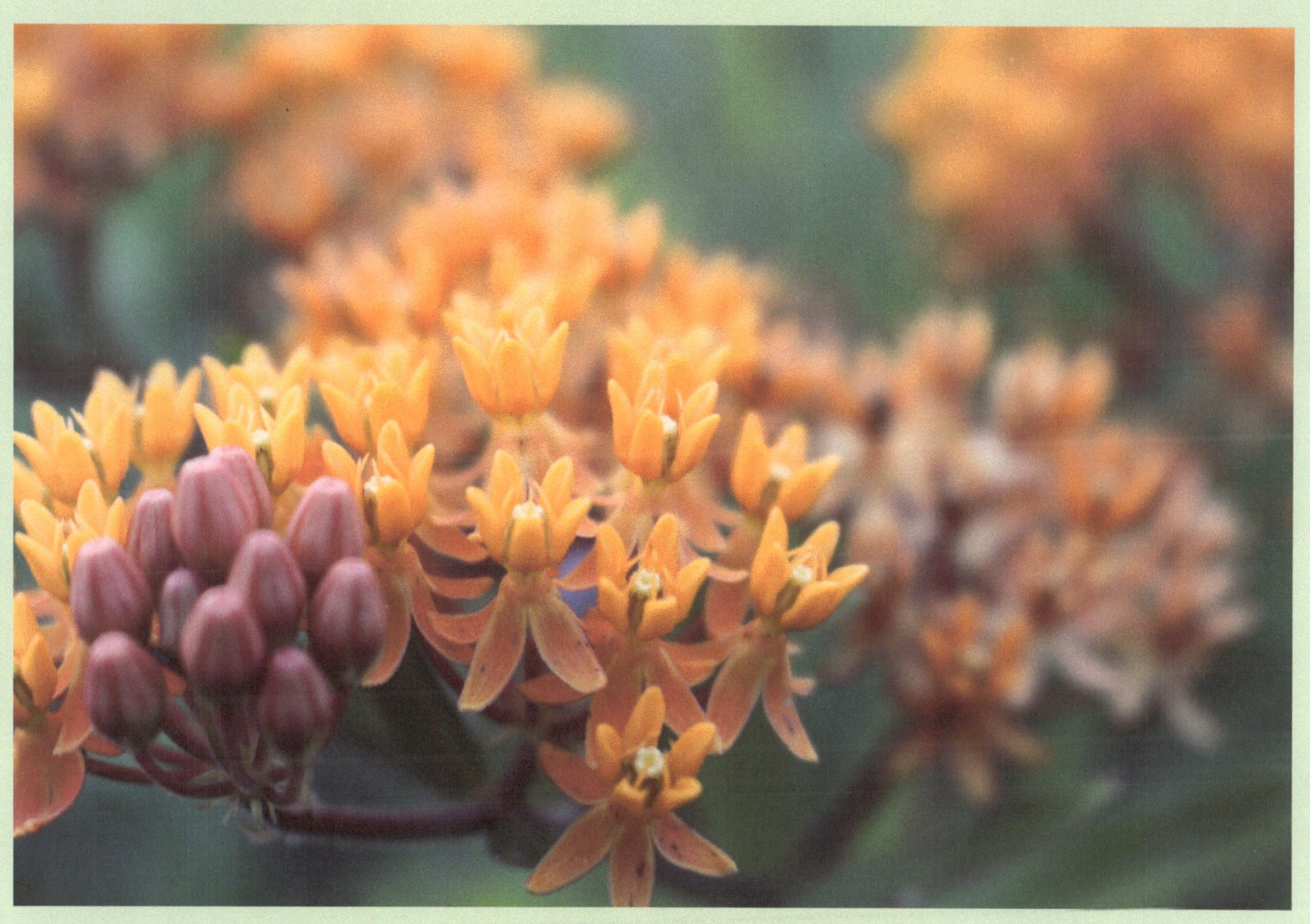

Photographer: Sarah Cashmore

26 acres dedicated in 2006

This property provides a scenic overview of sedge meadow and oak savanna, with Wonder Lake itself in the background. Thanks to the easement, generations to come will be able to stand here and enjoy the same scenic vista.

# Wilson Conservation Easement, Lake in the Hills
## *First Place Award*

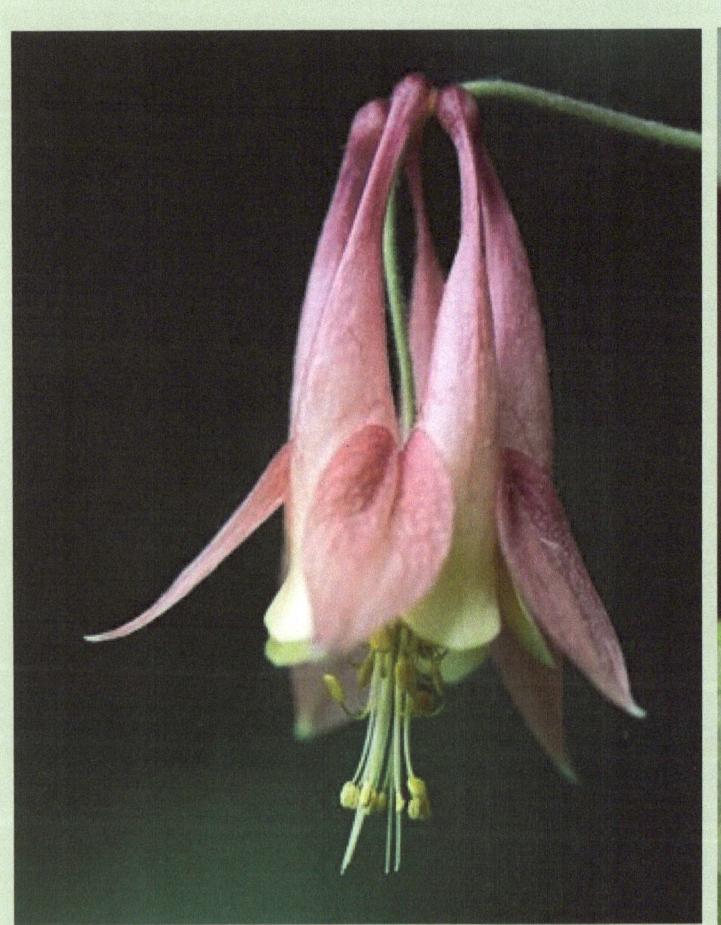
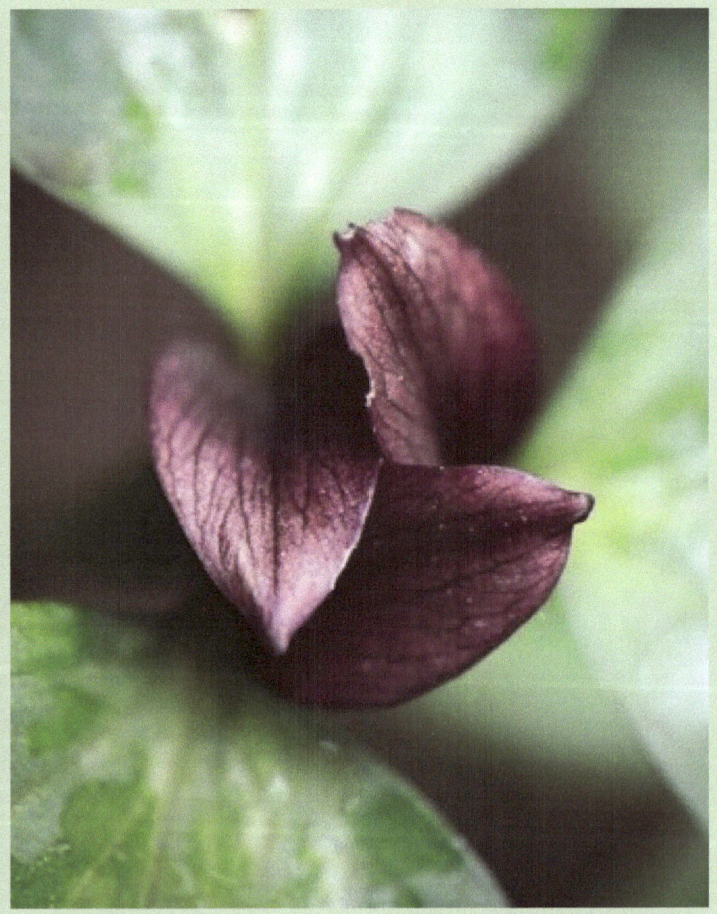

Lisa Meinhard-Sly's three photos of spring wildflowers taken at the Wilson Conservation Easement property in Lake in the Hills impressed the contest judges so much that they selected the three together as the winning "photo" in the 2015 contest. That is why they are presented to-

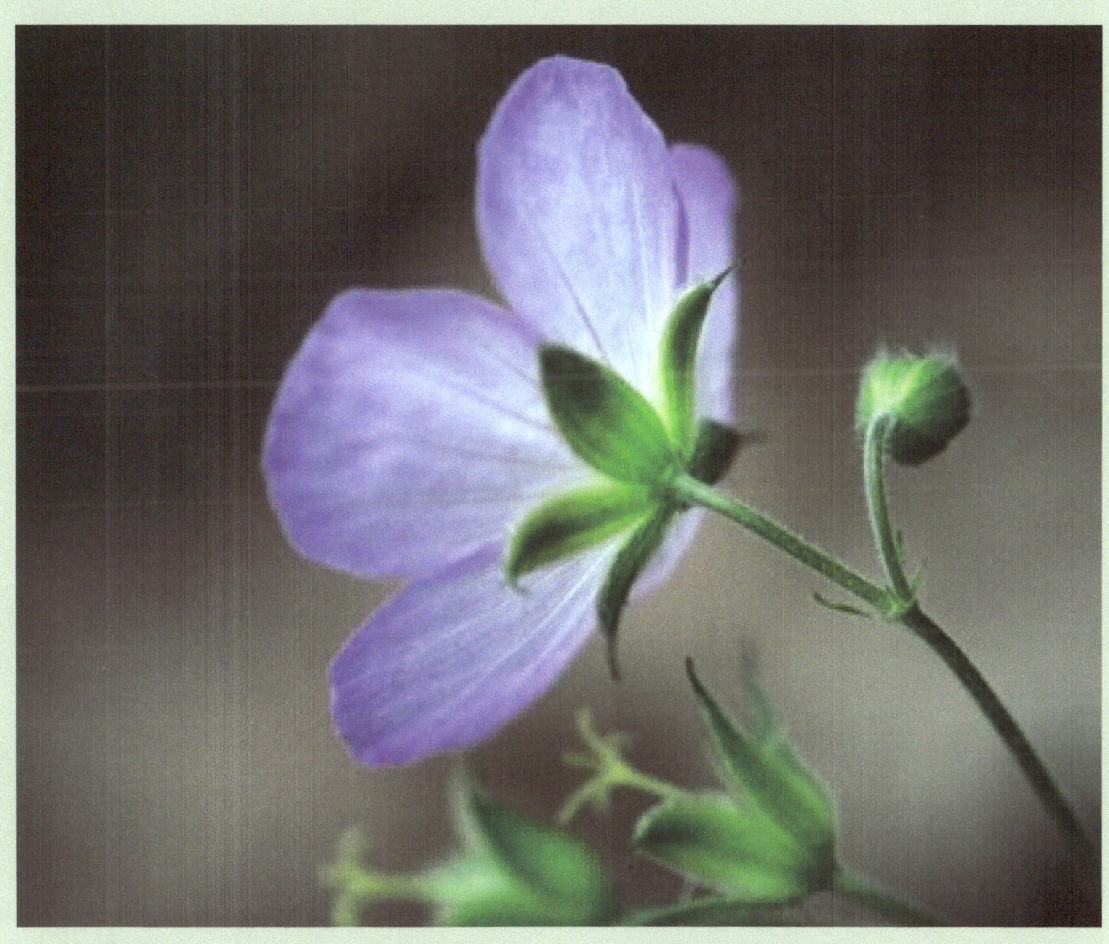

**Wilson Conservation Easement, Lake in the Hills**

**Photographer:  Lisa Meinhard-Sly**

**2 acres dedicated in 1999**

Barb & Al Wilson have lovingly tended the oak woodland on their property for many years, restoring a high level of biodiversity. The month of May greets them with an awesome display of the many spring ephemeral plants that were once common in this area: wild columbine, trillium, wild geranium (pictured here), and many more all thriving beneath the canopy of oaks that are more than 100 years old.

# Woodland Hills Conservation Easement, Lakewood

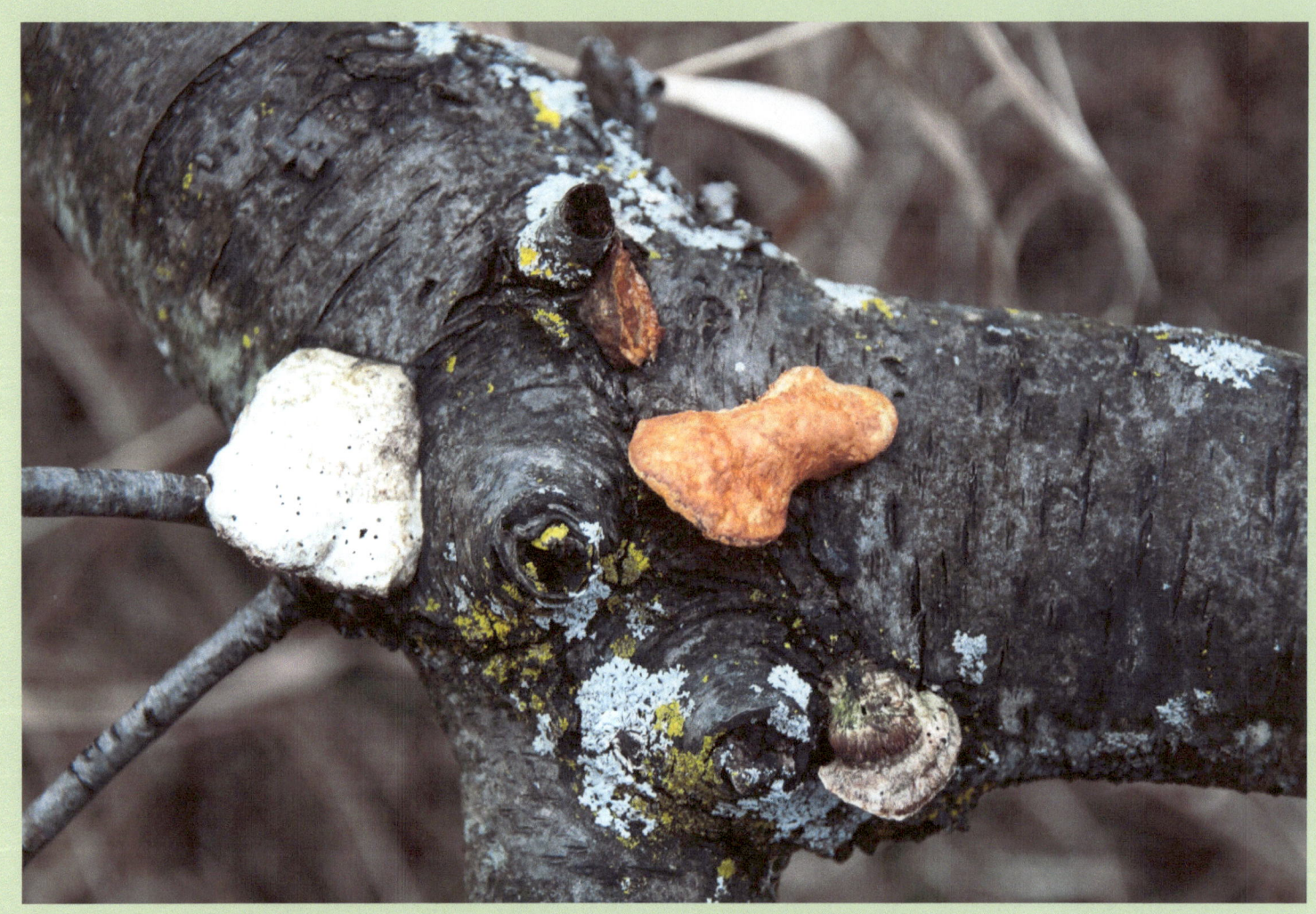

Photographer: Meg Struttman
58 acres dedicated in 2007

Near the corner of Ballard & Haligus Roads in Lakewood lies a 58 acre wetland and oak woods tucked in behind the Woodland Hills subdivision. While the surrounding development project has stalled with the economy, the wetland is as busy as ever providing critical habitat for birds, insects and local wildlife – and because of the conservation easement that the Village of Lakewood required, it will be available for nature forever!

# TLC's Art of the Land Photo Contest

Each year since 2009, TLC invites amateur photographers to participate in a unique photo contest meant to highlight the inspiring nature of its land preservation work. The contest's goal is to introduce more local residents to the work of TLC and the beauty found in even small natural areas when one stops long enough to look.

TLC matches each photographer with a specific TLC property, providing them with the opportunity to visit the site throughout multiple seasons of the year. All photographs submitted are taken of properties on which TLC holds a conservation easement, land TLC owns or stewards, or of people who work with TLC for the purpose of preserving their land for the benefit of future generations.

For more information about Art of the Land, the Photo Contest, or The Land Conservancy, please visit www.ConserveMC.org.

**TLC's 2015 Photo Contest was sponsored by Hey and Associates of Volo, Illinois. Thank you!**

# Information about TLC's 2015
# Art of the Land Art Sale and Benefit

2015 was the seventh year for TLC's Art of the Land Art Sale and Benefit at the Starline Factory in Harvard. This two-night event, held in September, is a collaboration between artists from the region who find inspiration in the land and McHenry County's oldest non-profit land conservation organization: The Land Conservancy of McHenry County.

Art of the Land could not happen without the many talented artists who participate, and without the hundreds of guests who attend the event and purchase artwork. Thirty percent of all sales go to support TLC's land preservation mission.

A big thank you goes to Orrin and Karen Kinney, owners of the Starline Factory, who donate use of the space to TLC for the benefit, and donate the labor of several workers to help set up the space for this unique show.

Finally we are eternally grateful to the many volunteers who donate hundreds of hours (valued at several thousand dollars) during the months leading up to the event. Volunteers do everything from hanging artwork, installing lighting, painting walls, serving food, selling tickets, sweeping floors, and coordinating live and silent auctions. Quite simply, Art of the Land could not happen without the efforts of all the volunteers.

**Please contact TLC about participating at a future event:**
**815-337-9502 or www.ConserveMC.org.**

www.ingramcontent.com/pod-product-compliance
Lightning Source LLC
Chambersburg PA
CBHW050410180526
45159CB00005B/2214